Religions and Religious Movements
SHINTO

Jeff Hay, Book Editor

Bonnie Szumski, Publisher, Series Editor
Helen Cothran, Managing Editor

GREENHAVEN PRESS
A part of Gale, Cengage Learning

GALE
CENGAGE Learning

Detroit • New York • San Francisco • New Haven, Conn • Waterville, Maine • London

© 2006 Gale, a part of Cengage Learning

For more information, contact
Greenhaven Press
27500 Drake Rd.
Farmington Hills, MI 48331-3535
Or you can visit our Internet site at gale.cengage.com

Cover credit: © Chris Rainier/CORBIS
© Corel Corporation, 38, 51, 177
© Corbis, 60
© Digital Stock, 78
Library of Congress, 86, 120, 132, 163, 198

LIBRARY OF CONGRESS CATALOGING-IN-PUBLICATION DATA

Shinto / Jeff Hay, book editor.
   p. cm. — (Religions and religious movements)
Includes bibliographical references and index.
ISBN 0-7377-2575-3 (lib. : alk. paper)
   1. Shinto—History. I. Hay, Jeff. II. Series.
BL2218. S524 2006
299.5'61—dc22   2005046299

Printed in the United States of America
2 3 4 5 6 7 12 11 10 09 08

$\mathscr{C}$*ontents*

thinkers to refine their theology, a long process which began in the twelfth century and continued into Japan's Tokugawa era (1600–1868).

istic in the 1930s, when Japan's territorial ambitions exploded into full-scale war.

Foreword

"Religion . . . is not really what is grasped by the brain. It is a heart grasp."
—Mohandas Gandhi

The impulse toward religion—to move beyond the world as we know it and ponder the larger questions of why we are here, whether there is a God who directs our lives, and how we should live—seems as universally human as breathing.

Yet, although this impulse is universal, different religions and their adherents are often at odds due to conflicts that stem from their opposing belief systems. These conflicts can also occur because many people have only the most tentative understanding of religions other than their own. In a time when religion seems to be at the root of growing tensions around the world, its study seems particularly relevant.

We live in a religiously diverse world. And while the world's many religions have coexisted for millennia, only recently, with information shared so easily and travel to even the most remote regions made possible for larger numbers of people, has this fact been fully acknowledged. It is no longer possible to ignore other religions, regardless of whether one views these religions positively or negatively.

The study of religion has also changed a great deal in recent times. Just a few decades ago in the United States, few students were exposed to any religion other than Christianity. Today, the study of religion reflects the pluralism of American society and the world at large. Religion courses and even current events classes focus on non-Christian religions as well as the religious experiences of groups that have in the past been marginalized by traditional Christianity, such as women and racial minorities.

In fact, the study of religion has been integrated into many different types of classes and disciplines. Anthropology, psychology, sociology, history, philosophy, political science, economics, and other fields often include discussions about different nations' religions and beliefs.

The study of religion involves so many disciplines because, for many cultures, it is integrated into many different parts of life. This point is often highlighted when American companies conduct business deals in Middle Eastern countries and inadvertently offend a host country's religious constrictions, for example. On both a small scale, such as personal travel, and on a large scale, such as international trade and politics, an understanding of the world's religions has become essential.

The goals of the Religions and Religious Movements series are several. The first is to provide students a historical context for each of the world's religions. Each book focuses on one religion and explores, through primary and secondary sources, its fundamental belief system, religious works of importance, and prominent figures. By using articles from a variety of sources, each book provides students with different theological and historical contexts for the religion.

The second goal of the series is to explore the challenges that each religion faces today. All of these religions are experiencing challenges and changes—some theological, some political—that are forcing alterations in attitude and belief. By reading about these current dilemmas, students will come to understand that religions are not abstract concepts, but a vital part of peoples' lives.

The last and perhaps most important objective is to make students aware of the wide variety of religious beliefs, as well as the factors, common to all religions. Every religion attempts to puzzle out essential questions as well as provide a model for doing good in the world. By using the books in the Religions and Religious Movements series, students will find that people with divergent, closely held beliefs may learn to live together and work toward the same goals.

Introduction

The Shinto religion is inseparable from the history of Japan, and its echoes appear in some of the nation's most decisive moments. In 1274 Japan faced an invasion from the Mongols and their great warlord Kublai Khan. The Mongols had already conquered a huge empire, stretching from central Europe in the west to China and Korea in the east. They were feared everywhere for their war skills and brutality. The major factor that had prevented a prior invasion of Japan, a rich and sophisticated civilization, was that Japan was a nation of islands and the Mongols were unskilled in seamanship. Still, Mongol generals were confident that Japan, like so many other nations, would fall to their armies.

Their invasion failed due to poor weather in the Sea of Japan, the waterway separating the Japanese islands from the Asian mainland. A second invasion attempt in 1281 also failed. This time, after heavy fighting along the coast of Kyushu, Japan's southernmost major island, an intense storm once again dispersed and then scuttled much of the Mongol fleet. Kublai Khan was said to have lost half of his invasion force of 140,000 men.

Divine Winds

The Japanese attributed their two victories to kamikaze, or divine winds. By this they meant that the *kami*, or gods, had whipped up powerful storms in order to save the Japanese people against what was then the greatest army on Earth. Later, in World War II in the 1940s, the Japanese once again called on kamikaze to help them defeat the United States. This time, however, the kamikaze were human, pilots who used their sometimes damaged aircraft as bombs against American ships. The divine element in this case was within the pilots themselves, who were prepared to commit suicide for the greater glory of Japan.

The *kami* of the Mongol era and of World War II were reflections of Shinto, the traditional religion of Japan. Shinto is an animistic religion, claiming that all life and all natural forces are animated by a divine spirit. The *kami*, most simply, are specific manifestations or interpretations of this divine spirit, such as the winds that dispersed the Mongol fleets. But the *kami* might also be household or guardian spirits or even deified humans such as past Japanese emperors. There are so many of them, and they are so pervasive, that Shinto must be considered a fundamental part of the Japanese way of life. *Kami* can be seen everywhere, from the cycle of annual harvests to the rites and ceremonies practiced by Japanese people today in order to encourage unity and prosperity.

Although Shinto was the first Japanese religion, it is not the only one. Japan, in fact, provides an example of religious syncretism, where various religions have meshed and overlapped, and Japanese people are quite comfortable with this arrangement. Aside from Shinto, the main religion of Japan is Buddhism, imported from China and Korea (which had in turn imported it from India) in the fifth and sixth centuries. Other Chinese imports included Confucianism and Taoism (pronounced "dow-ism"). Confucianism was particularly influential. It is a social philosophy as much as a religion, preaching the need for earthly harmony achieved through observing social hierarchies and by following proper rituals concerned with such matters as filial, or family, piety. Taoism is more abstract, emphasizing harmony with nature and the universe.

Since the sixteenth century, and despite periods of repression, many Japanese have adopted Christianity as an alternative to these faiths. And in more modern times a complex group of "new religions" have become popular in Japan. Many are based on Shinto or Buddhism, but a number of the new religions are distinct enough to be considered completely new faiths. Adopting Christianity or one of the new religions does not necessarily mean that one rejects Shinto. The religion is simply too much a part of Japanese history and culture. It is practiced by groups of Japanese immigrants in North and South America, most notably in Hawaii, California, and Brazil, but Shinto is most closely associated with the 125 million people who live in Japan.

Shinto's Beginnings in Ancient Japan

Shinto's origins are mysterious. The faith does not have a founder comparable to the Buddha or Jesus of Nazareth, nor does it have an acknowledged set of texts like the Bible or Koran. It is perhaps most accurately described as a set of folk customs and beliefs that evolved into an organized religion. Even then, however, what united Shinto believers were a few broad ideas and a sense of the presence of the *kami*. Modes of worship such as specific rituals or festivals are and have always been numerous and varied. One of the few generalizations that can be safely made is that Shinto practice is based on the presence of a shrine, a spot where the earthly can connect with the divine. Permanent shrines usually are entered through a torii, an arched gateway that symbolizes the meeting point between the two. In Japanese tradition the word *jinja* is used to denote a Shinto shrine while *tera* is the term for a Buddhist temple. The custom is followed in English. Shrines are Shinto centers while temples are Buddhist ones, when speaking of Japanese religion.

By the time the first written records of Japanese history appeared in the eighth century, there was already a settled urban civilization in Japan, and the overlapping of Shinto and Buddhism had begun. These early chronicles, the *Nihongi* (or *Nihon shoki*) and *Kojiki*, were written in Chinese characters and are primarily accounts of Japan's founding myths and the origins of the leading clans as well as the early history of the kingdom.

The *Nihongi* claims that Japan appeared during a prehistoric "age of the gods." Then, generations of invisible *kami* emerged out of a formless chaos. During the eighth generation of these invisible deities two *kami*, Izanagi and Izanami, created the first land by dipping a spear into the formless mass that made up the earth. After descending to this land, Izanami was tricked into going to Yomi, the land of the dead. After failing to rescue her, Izanagi purified himself of the defilement of Yomi by bathing in a river. While doing so, three new *kami* were born from his two eyes and his nose, the figurative "children" of Izanagi and Izanami. They were the sun goddess Amaterasu, the moon god Tsukiyomi, and the storm god Susano. Izanagi in time retired, making Amaterasu the supreme deity while Tsukiyomi became the lord of the night and Susano the lord of the sea. Other stories note how Amaterasu and Susano quarrelled, and in so doing produced other *kami*, some of whom were to be the progenitors of Japan's main clans. For various misdoings Susano was ultimately banished from heaven while Tsukiyomi remained within his realm. Amaterasu was left as the greatest of all the *kami*. The age of the gods came to an end when her legendary human descendant, Jimmu Tenno, took the throne as Japan's first emperor around 660 B.C. and the imperial line, still in existence, was established.

These chronicles have been balanced against archaelogical research, which notes that during Japan's Yayoi period (250 B.C.–A.D. 250), certain elements of Shinto had already begun to appear, such as the imperial symbols, and the signs of the favor of the kami: the sword, jewel, and mirror. Other elements include the prominence of *ujigami*, or guardian clan spirits, and a concern with fertility. The latter was particularly understandable given the importance to Japan of rice growing: Many Shinto festivals to this day are connected to the rice crop, and each new emperor is enthroned with a ritual known as *daijosai*, in which he consumes specially grown new rice.

By the sixth century the Yamato clan had established its authority over much of the central part of the country. The Yamato legitimized their rule by claiming descent from Amaterasu, cementing the connection between Japanese leadership and the Shinto *kami*. This relationship waxed and waned over the centuries, but it never entirely disappeared. In the same era Buddhism began to arrive, brought by Chinese and Korean missionaries, and it proved particularly attractive to Japan's ruling elites, who wanted to adopt the more sophisticated civilizations of their neighbors. Nevertheless leaders never rejected Shinto, and a sometimes uneasy reconciliation of the two faiths began. This is sometimes referred to as *ryobu Shinto*, or "double Shinto," and it continued for centuries.

Shinto and Buddhism

The reconciliation of Shinto with Buddhism began in earnest during Japan's Heian period (794–1185), when Japanese elites developed a sophisticated culture based in the city of Kyoto. It continued even after militaristic leaders from powerful clans replaced the emperors as the true rulers of Japan. These new leaders took the title of shogun, or "emperor's military adviser," and they dominated Japan until 1867. During these centuries Japan could be an unstable and violent place, but its distinct civilization continued to emerge. One feature of this period, Japan's so-called middle ages, was the rise of a class of warriors known as samurai. The samurai were not only skilled fighters, they were trained in a very strict code of etiquette, part of which was to show due reverence toward all religions.

One popular Shinto deity among the samurai was Hachiman, the *kami* of war and battle. Hachiman was often praised in Buddhist temples as well as Shinto shrines, and the various modes of Hachiman worship provide only one example of *ryobu* Shinto in these centuries. In its most basic form double Shinto was concerned with the true nature of the *kami*. Shinto spirits like Amaterasu or Hachiman were described by Buddhists as bodhisattvas, or "little Buddhas." In Buddhism bodhisattvas are souls who have achieved enlightenment, the ultimate goal of all Buddhists, but instead of entering the Buddhist state of nonbeing and bliss known as nirvana, bodhisattvas remain accessible to mortals to provide aid and assistance. This description was easily grasped by Shintoists, who believed that their *kami* can be easily called upon, in the proper place and with the proper rituals. Shintoists, indeed, sometimes returned the gesture by depicting the major Japanese bodhisattvas as Shinto *kami*. These included Jizo, the protector of sufferers; Kannon, the god (or often a goddess) of forgiveness; and Amida (actually a Buddha), who presides over the "western paradise" that believers in Pure Land Buddhism, Japan's most popular Buddhist sect, aspire to.

The bodhisattvas, who are called *bosatsu* in Japanese, have joined the most prominent Shinto *kami* as the most popular objects of religious devotion in Japan. In addition to Amaterasu and Hachiman, these include Inari, the rice god who is often associated with the fox; Daikokuten and Ebisu, who represent wealth and material prosperity; and Jurojin, the *kami* of long life and health.

Despite this overlapping, there remained important differences between Shinto and Buddhism, and during the middle ages and after, Shinto thinkers often tried to emphasize these differences as part of an effort to retain the distinctness of Shinto. One difference, relating again to the nature of the *kami*, was that the Buddhist *bosatsu* were invariably benevolent and generous. The Shinto *kami*, on the other hand, had both kind and dangerous aspects, known respectively as *nigimitama* and *aramitama*. Both were manifestations of *tama*, the life force whose emanations can be both beneficial and harmful as well as unpredictable. Shinto worship often emphasized the effort to draw forth the *nigimitama* of a particular deity, or to minimize or reduce the *arami-*

tama in order to draw on life's benefits while mitigating its dangers. Because of this difference, some Shintoists considered their faith to be more essential, more true to life, than Buddhism, which they found otherworldly and abstract. It is also reflected in the fact that many Japanese people perform Shinto ceremonies when they are concerned with earthly matters such the harvest or health and Buddhist ones when concerned with death and the afterlife.

Shinto's Emphasis on Earthly Life

Some Shinto thinkers went further, questioning the importance of Buddhism because it was a foreign import, a way of thought not native to Japan, while Shinto was not only inseparable from Japanese history, the *kami* could be found in almost every feature of the Japanese landscape from the "divine winds" in the Sea of Japan to the sacred Mount Fuji near Tokyo to the springtime cherry blossoms that inspire yearly celebrations. This way of thinking was most prominent during a seventy-five-year period of Japanese history lasting from 1868 to 1945. During these years Japan transformed itself quickly into a global economic and military power. It was quite a contrast from the preceding era, the period of the Tokugawa shoguns (1600–1868), when Japan was almost entirely closed off from outside influences.

The transformation began in 1853, when American naval ships arrived off the Japanese coast demanding trading and diplomatic privileges. The Americans were soon followed by the British, French, and other Western powers. In response to this onslaught, Japanese reformist leaders seized control of the government and installed, after the abdication of the last Tokugawa shogun, a new emperor, the Meiji emperor. The age of the shoguns was over, and Japan's ambitious new leaders decided to use Shinto to help them build a unified, modern nation. Shinto, they believed, made Japan different from other nations, more homogeneous, more united in purpose, and when necessary, stronger. A new "state Shinto" arose in which Shinto priests were deemed government employees, while the government itself devised various offices to direct Shinto affairs. Buddhism, the faith of foreign origin, was marginalized. Leaders argued, confusingly, that Shinto was not a state religion, instead, state Shinto was merely an approach to national organization. Indeed, the constitution of 1889 proclaimed that Japan was a nation of complete religious freedom. Ordinary Shintoists, meanwhile, found it difficult to maintain the proper sense of separation, especially when Shinto ideas appeared in school textbooks and visits to shrines became occasions for nationalist activity as well as worship.

State Shinto and Emperor Worship

The key feature of this new state Shinto was the revival of belief in the divine nature of the emperor. Japanese leaders encouraged people to remember that their imperial line was the oldest on Earth, that the present emperor was the descendant of the first one, Jimmu Tenno, who was in turn the descendant of the sun goddess Amaterasu. The emperor was to be an object of true religious devotion, not merely respect; ordinary people were expected to bow their heads on the rare occasions when he appeared in public and passed them. When the Meiji emperor died in 1912 he was officially "deified" by Shinto authorities, turned into a true god, and the shrine built in his honor in Tokyo was one of the largest in Japan. In 1940, when Meiji's grandson Hirohito, the Showa emperor, was on the throne, the nation celebrated the twenty-six-hundredth anniversary of the accession to the throne of Jimmu Tenno. It was an occasion of much militant nationalism, because Japan was then at war.

Already in possession of Korea and Taiwan, Japan invaded Manchuria, north of China, in 1931. This was followed by a full-scale invasion of China in 1937. With a strong faith in their racial and cultural superiority supported at least in part by state Shinto, Japan wanted to dominate Asia, to establish what they called a "greater East Asia coprosperity sphere" in which Japanese industries would call upon the labor and resources of the rest of the continent. The year 1941 saw moves into such

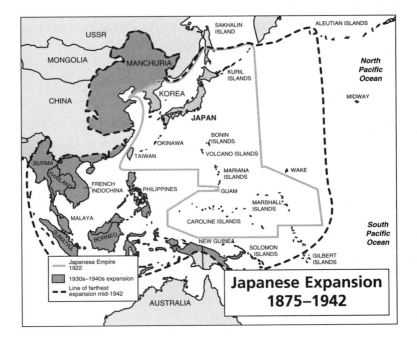

Japanese Expansion 1875–1942

Southeast Asian nations as Thailand and Burma (now Myanmar), and in order to prevent American forces from hindering their ambitions, Japanese aircraft bombed, in a surpise attack on December 7, 1941, the U.S. naval base at Pearl Harbor in Hawaii.

The ensuing war between the United States and its allies and Japan ended in August 1945, in an utter disaster for Japan. Most of its cities were in rubble even before atomic bombs fell on Hiroshima and Nagasaki early that month, and people were starving. It fell, in fact, to Hirohito to commit Japan to an unconditional surrender to end the war; most of his politicians and generals were unable to accept the humiliation. When the emperor announced the surrender over the radio on August 15, it was the first time most Japanese people had ever heard his voice. In the effort to restore spiritual balance, one of the last, if informal, gestures of state Shinto was left to some of the ordinary Japanese who flocked to the emperor's palace after hearing the surrender announcement; they committed seppuku, or ritual suicide.

Ending State Shinto After World War II

American and other allied forces occupied Japan from 1945 until 1952 and officially dismantled state Shinto. It was among their first efforts to reconstruct a peaceful Japan, and it was based on the fundamental American belief in the need to separate church and state. Arguing that state Shinto contributed to Japan's aggressive nationalism, occupation officials severed most ties between the state and Shinto shrines and marginalized those voices that had proclaimed that Shinto reflected the superiority of Japanese culture. School textbooks and other media products based on Shinto nationalism were banned. Hirohito, for his part, proved ready to accept the new circumstances. He formally renounced in 1946 the claim that he was divine.

After the American occupation ended, Japan returned to its familiar pattern of religious syncretism. This is most clearly visible on the local level; whether in towns or cities, Japanese people form lasting attachments to the religious institutions that stand nearby. These might be Shinto shrines or Buddhist temples and, commonly, people visit both. Again, the Japanese religious sense is formed on the basis of the existence of spirits that animate all natural life, a Shinto idea. Whether these spirits take Shinto or Buddhist names is simply a matter of tradition, preference, or the emphasis of a particular ritual. Some Japanese, notably groups of Protestant Christians and followers of some of the "new religions" such as Tenrikyo ("Heavenly Truth"), cling to their faiths alone without any overlap from Shinto or Buddhism. But most people continue to adhere to the long Japanese tradition of religious openness.

More Women as Shrine Priests

Shinto has also adapted to suit changing social and economic conditions in Japan. Shrines, for instance, have become more and more willing to install female priests, despite opposition from social conservatives. By the late 1990s some 10 percent of all shrine priests were women. In addition, women have been increasingly allowed to carry the *mikoshi*, or portable shrines, used in Shinto processions; traditionally this has been a privilege limited to men. Women's roles in Shinto worship, therefore, have grown far more extensive than the support roles characterized by the *miko*, or unmarried female shrine attendants, of other eras. While the *miko* still exist, many of them are simply adopting the role during festivals or ceremonies, taking a break from their everyday lives as students or office workers. Shrines themselves, meanwhile, are community centers. They offer not only places of worship but sites for community activities and places where, in the fast-paced, crowded Japan of today, people can find quiet and solace and, when necessary or appropriate, worship in their own ways. Meanwhile, the Shinto tradition of portable and temporary shrines continues in ways suitable to modern life. Offices or shops might contain small shrines devoted to Inari or one of the other major *kami*, while roadside shrines offer worship opportunities to travelers. A major new innovation is the online, Internet Shinto shrine, the Sakura Jinja, based on the Sakura shrine in Tokyo.

Innovations and Controversies

Some longstanding traditions remain alive, and some of these are controversial. Since the Heian era, for instance, it has been customary to simultaneously tear down and rebuild the great Shinto shrines at Ise (the outer shrine is dedicated to the harvest deity Toyouke, the inner shrine is dedicated to Amaterasu) every twenty years, although events have occasionally altered the timetable. The last such reconstruction occurred in 1993. Much more controversial is the status of the Yasukuni shrine in Tokyo. During the nineteenth century it evolved into a national shrine to honor those killed in war, and it retains that status today, with important politicians frequently visiting to pay their respects. The shrine's museum memorializes the kamikaze pilots of World War II as well as other nationalist sacrifices. Some Shintoists, as well as Japanese nationalists, believe that Yasukuni should receive extensive support from the state. Others fear that such support might signal a return to the state Shinto of the imperialist years and prefer that government and religion remain separate even here.

This, however, is a matter of official policy, not of longstanding Shinto-based customs and traditions, which remain inseparable from Japanese life. The springtime renewal of life is cause for annual celebrations, most famously when the cherry blossoms, a symbol of fertility and nature's bounty, bloom. Japanese emperors, meanwhile, still adhere to many Shinto customs and some people believe that the emperor is the chief priest of all Shinto shrines. When Hirohito died and was dubbed the Showa emperor (emperors take the name of their period of reign after their death), he was buried according to Shinto rites. To protect the principle of the separation of church and state, however, these rites were performed away from the public eye. The current emperor, Akihito, was likewise enthroned according to Shinto rites. These included the *daijosai*, the great thanksgiving ceremony in which the new emperor, as his predecessors had for centuries, consumed specially grown rice as a symbol of his communion with Amaterasu, the sun goddess who, according to legend, was the founder of the Japanese imperial line.

CHAPTER 1

Early Shinto

Shinto's Origins in Early Japan

by David S. Noss and John B. Noss

The Shinto religion is associated with Japan, the East Asian nation comprising four major islands (and numerous smaller ones) that is today one of the world's great economic and cultural powers with a population of some 125 million. In the following selection religious scholars David S. Noss and John B. Noss describe how Shinto emerged slowly, in parallel with the rise of an advanced civilization in the Japanese islands. This process began in the first millennium B.C., but since written records for the era do not exist and archaeological evidence is inconclusive, scholars have found it difficult to pinpoint an exact beginning for Shinto. Believers trace the start of the faith to a mythical era known in Japanese chronicles as the Age of the Gods. The first date of earthly importance in the Shinto calendar is the beginning of the reign of Jimmu Tenno, the first Japanese emperor, in approximately 660 B.C.

The authors note that Shinto only begins to be coherent with the arrival of Chinese influences, usually by way of Korea, the peninsula between China and Japan. As Chinese and Korean officials and travelers arrived in Japan from the fifth century A.D. onward, they brought with them many aspects of their cultures, notably the Chinese written language. Indeed, the first written records of Japanese history were written using Chinese characters, and *Shinto* itself is derived from a Chinese word. Chinese influences also helped the early Japanese evolve toward a settled, urban civilization, based at first on two important families, the Izumo and Yamato. The Yamato were particularly important emperors of Japan during its first period of "official" or written history, the Nara period, lasting from 710 to 794. The authors assert that the Yamato claimed descent from the Shinto sun goddess Amaterasu, who emerged as the most revered of all the Shinto deities. David S. Noss is professor of religion at Heidelberg College. The late John B. Noss was professor of religion at Franklin and Marshall College and author of *Man's Religions*, a commonly used textbook for four decades.

The word *Shinto* is derived from the Chinese *shendao*, meaning "the way of the higher spirits or gods." Its equivalent in Japanese is *kami-no-michi* or "the kami's way," *kami* meaning in general gods or deities, but, in a more inclusive sense, also beings possessing sacred power or superior potency, filled with a numinous [spiritual] or charismatic force. It has been part of the myth of Shinto that Japan was once peopled exclusively with kami. The early Japanese regarded the whole of nature as imbued with kami-powers, from the gods in the upper regions to spirits in mountains, lakes, and trees on earth, not to speak of powers in the sea and under the ground. Shinto thus expresses a religious faith about Japan and its past. The customs of prehistoric Japan were the way followed by kami, the awe-inspiring beings from whom the Japanese people have descended. But this faith, as faiths often do, ignored or was unaware of certain historical facts about the true origins of the Japanese people.

Ethnic Origins

The Japanese are probably a mixed people, partly Korean, partly Mongolian, and partly Malayan. Their ancestors came at different times from the Asiatic mainland and South Pacific islands, and succeeded in uniting with or displacing and driving northward the aboriginal tribes. Apparently, the civil condition of ancient Japan was that of a loose conjunction of tribes and clans, each more or less independent and with its own traditions of nature- and chieftain-worship. Magic, taboo, and religion were commingled in the fashion that is characteristic of a primitive society. The fox was worshiped as a messenger of the gods. Bows and arrows were fetishes of so high an order that they were offered the reverence accorded to the gods. The constant warfare with the slowly yielding but still fierce aboriginal tribesmen gave a military color to the whole of life. Great warriors were treated with special respect, whether living or dead.

Though they were clothed in rough garments, and primitively housed, the Japanese already showed the passion for personal cleanliness that is so characteristic of them today. Their attitude toward the dead was marked by a dread of pollution, so that when a death occurred, the funeral was immediately held, and after the ten-day mourning period was at an end, the whole family went into the water to wash. In many cases the survivors abandoned the primitive structure that had been the home of the dead person and built a new one.

Prehistoric Cultures

Archaeology yields only the sketchiest of chronologies of prehistoric Japan. Surviving pottery dating possibly from as early as 6000 B.C. and still in use at 300 B.C. has a "cord pattern" that has given its name to the time in which it was in use, the *Jomon* period. This seems to have been a long Neolithic hunting and fishing period, when aboriginal tribes inhabited the land. Their relics imply ritual burials, with the dead interred in a flexed position along with stone implements and red ochre; there seem also to have been fertility rites in which phallic emblems (stone clubs) and clay figurines of indeterminate sex were used. The name of a district near Tokyo, where another and more advanced type of pottery has been found, is attributed to the *Yayoi* period (250 B.C. to [A.D.] 250). Apparently it was during this period that cultivation of rice in irrigated paddy fields was developed, an important advance over the gathering practices of earlier times. Historians have coined yet a third term, the *Kofun* or Tomb period, to name the time from 250 to the historic breakthrough of Chinese influence in the fifth century. During this period tombs and earthen mausoleums were erected for the ruling classes, a fact that suggests to some scholars a large-scale invasion by Asiatic warriors, who brought with them the horse and the art of smelting bronze and iron and who drove the aborigines farther northward. The earliest Chinese records go back to this period, and they tell of able women ruling in south Japan and acting as influential shamans there.

There were, it seems likely, three main centers of culture about the time of the first century B.C.: one in the southwest on the island of Kyushu, another at Izumo, on the western verge of the main island [Honshu] and

a third at Yamato, at the northern end of the Inland
Sea. Far to the north were the light-skinned Ainu, originally from the subarctic areas of Siberia, who doggedly
preserved their own cultural life down through the
years. (They are now in Hokkaido [Japan's northern-
most major island].) It may be an oversimplification,
but there are indications that on the island of Kyushu
the tribal cults were mainly concerned with gods of the
sea, and upon the central island the Izumo clans worshiped the storm-god Susa-no-wo [or Susano], while
the Yamato clans adored the sun-goddess [Amaterasu]
regarded as the ruler of the heavens and the ancestress
of their chieftains. The Yamato clans, probably in the
fourth century, sealed their ascendancy over the other
groups by placing their chieftain on a somewhat shaky
imperial throne as a descendant of the sun. But perhaps
they had to overcome the opposition of other groups
who preferred as rulers women reigning in the matriar-
chal tradition and credited with special powers as di-
viners and shamanistic mediums.

The Effect of Chinese Culture

However arrived at, primitive Shinto was formless and
without any particular sense of direction. It became a
clearly worked-out pattern of national culture only
when Chinese civilizing influences began to operate in
Japan in the fifth century A.D. These influences were
initially Sino-Korean, for the immediate teachers of the
Japanese were Koreans. But because the Koreans had
learned from the Chinese, the Japanese were not long
in going directly to the Chinese for further advances in
knowledge and skills. The transformation effected then
in the national life and outlook is one of the most re-

markable instances of its kind in history. The Japanese eagerly made their lives over by adapting Chinese ideas and procedures to their needs. They went about it very thoroughly.

Always adept in improving their methods and skills in the practical arts, once the way is shown, they quickly learned all that the Koreans and beyond them the Chinese could teach them about metalworking, wood carving, farming, horticulture, gardening, silk-worm culture, road and bridge building, and canal dredging. Almost at a bound the people passed from a primitive to a relatively advanced type of material culture. In the realm of writing and communication, they took over without change, except for cursive simplifications, the entire body of Chinese ideograms or characters, pronouncing them with the Japanese words that were the translations of the Chinese. Where there were no Japanese equivalents they adopted the Chinese sounds with characteristic modifications. In the realm of social relations, Confucian ideas [derived from the work of the Chinese philosopher Confucius (551–479 B.C.)] brought about permanent changes of emphasis in morals. There followed in particular a powerful reenforcement of the ideal of filial piety. Prehistoric Shinto had been mainly a haphazard cult of nature-worship, loosely tied in with ancestor-worship. It now took on the aspects of history's most comprehensive ancestor-cult. Not only did the emperor's descent from the sun-goddess receive stress, but the higher officials began to trace their own descent from the deities most closely related to the sun-goddess, and the common people were supposed to be descendants of the more distantly related deities. In this way the mythological basis was laid for the claim (so greatly emphasized during the last decades of the nineteenth century and the beginning of [the twentieth]) that the whole people were organically related to the emperor by a divine family relationship.

Early Sacred Literature

But an even greater impact was made upon the Japanese by Buddhism, coming first by way of Korea and then from China. When this religion came to Japan in the sixth century, it brought with it an exciting literature, a new, rich art, an emotionally satisfying ritual, and fresh insights in every field of human thought and action, including logic, medicine, and social service. Buddhism broke down Japanese provincialism by bringing the overseas world into the religious picture, for in the eyes of Buddhist priests, the seats of religious insight and authority lay not in Japan, but in India and China. Buddhism had so much to contribute to Japan that the country's best, most progressive minds were irresistibly attracted to it.

One important result of the new ferment of ideas was the attempt, under imperial sanction, to use the Chinese characters and put into writing the native myths and traditions still current among the local clans. In 712 the *Kojiki*, or Chronicle of Ancient Events, was completed, it being intended as a history of Japan from the creation of the world to the middle of the seventh century. Paralleling it, with variations and additions that gave it greater historical accuracy, was the *Nihongi* or *Nihon Shoki*, "Chronicles of Japan," issued in 720. Almost a century later, about 806 during the first decade of the Heian era [794–1185] appeared the *Kogoshui*, or Gleanings from Ancient Stories, a defense of the practices of ancient priestly families connected with Shinto. Still later, in the first quarter of the tenth century, came the *Engi-shiki*, an important compendium of Shinto traditions in fifty parts, the first ten of which contain lists of ritual prayers or litanies for various ceremonial occasions, called *norito*. The norito served then and for centuries afterward as the models, if not the actual words, of prayers in all Shinto shrines, whether in the country at large or in the court. All these treatises showed the influence of Chinese and Buddhist ideas. Foreign modes of thought were evident, for example, in the opening paragraphs of the *Kojiki* and *Nihongi*, much as the influence of Greek philosophy on Christianity shows in the first chapter of the Fourth Gospel [of the Bible's New Testament]. The *Kojiki* and *Nihongi* were deeply indebted to overseas thought for their political orientation, which led them to endow the imperial line with a sovereignty reaching back to remote time and grounded in a divine order of things.

More undilutedly Japanese were two extraordinary works of the Heian period reflecting Japanese life, love, and religion. They came into being when Japanese minds were stirred to creativity by the exciting opportunity presented by the Chinese characters to put old and new thoughts into writing. One was the *Manyōshū*, a collection of old and new poems, four thousand in number, compiled toward the end of the eighth century. The other was a work of genius, Lady Murasaki's long novel *The Tale of Genji*, dealing with the sensuous, beauty-oriented court at Kyoto in its early years.

Gods, Rituals, and Beliefs of Early Shinto

by William K. Bunce

The following selection is taken from a text prepared by scholars attached to the American occupation government in Japan after World War II. Edited by William K. Bunce, the chief of the religions division of the occupation government, it describes the nature of Shinto belief as well as some of its early practices. Shinto is one of the few major modern religions that maintains clear elements of animism. Animism is the belief that a divine spirit animates everything on Earth, from humans to animals to objects such as mountains or trees. The divine spirit might also be seen in natural forces such as the wind, rain, or tides. In Shinto, the manifestations of this divine spirit are called *kami*, and the translation of the Japanese language term for Shinto, *kami-no-michi*, is the "way of the *kami*." As Japanese civilization evolved in the first millennium A.D., the worship of *kami* came to involve purification rituals, the use of objects to divert evil spirits and delineate sacred spots, and the construction of shrines. The entrance to a Shinto shrine, even today, is through a ritual gateway known as a torii, the dividing line between the earthly realm and the realm of the *kami*. As parts of Japan were centralized under the ruling Yamato clan,

William K. Bunce, *Religions in Japan: Buddhism, Shinto, Christianity.* Rutland, VT: Charles E. Tuttle Company, 1955. Copyright in Japan, 1955, by Charles E. Tuttle Co., Inc. All rights reserved. Reproduced by permission of the author.

the Yamato deity, Amaterasu the sun goddess, emerged as the most important of all *kami*. However, other clans continued to revere their own *kami*, as did ordinary Japanese people who were agricultural peasants, and Amaterasu was never the equivalent of the Christian God, the Islamic Allah, or the Hindu Vishnu or Shiva. Indeed, the nature of Shinto ensured, then and now, that the number of *kami* was limitless.

Religion in ancient Japan was a combination of animism and nature worship. All things animate or inanimate—people, objects, and natural phenomena—were believed to have souls or spirits and were apparently thought to possess the power of speech. This soul was the spiritual essence, that which gives life or activity to substance, even inanimate substance. Deities were called *kami*, and this term was applied to the deities of heaven and earth, to their spirits which dwelt in shrines, and to beasts, birds, plants, seas, mountains, and to such natural phenomena as storms, winds, and echoes. Apparently, the early Japanese worshipped the divine spirit in anything, whether noble or malignant, which seemed to possess extraordinary powers or qualities which evoked awe.

Kami is a word with such a variety of meanings that no truly accurate definition of it can he given. The literal translation of the character by which it is represented is "above," and it is generally used to imply superiority. When used to imply spiritual superiority, it may be permissible to translate it as "god," but it should be realized that, when used in this connection, it means to the Japanese an object of reverence rather than of worship in the Occidental [Western] sense. It is still a common word used to indicate, among other things, mere superiority of location or rank. The early Japanese applied it indiscriminately to any object, animate or inanimate, which was superior, mysterious, fearful, powerful, or incomprehensible. One must grasp this simple concept of deity if he is to understand the basic meaning of *kami*.

Man's approach to the *kami* was one of friendly intimacy. He felt love and gratitude and the desire to console or placate. Fear was almost totally absent. The idea of the soul and the distinctions between life and death—body and spirit—were extremely vague, however, and this early religion appears to have lacked speculative philosophical elements. There was little differentiation between worship of an object as a deity, worship of its spirit, and worship of its attributes. Life and growth were desirable; decay and death were evils to be avoided. Anthropomorphism [giving animals or inanimate objects human characteristics] was common but undeveloped.

There was hardly any ancestor worship in ancient Japan, and the bodies of the dead were treated with no special respect. One common method for disposing of bodies was to expose them in trees. Later, burial in mounds or tombs was adopted. If there was ancestor worship, it was probably known only to the ruling family and the upper class. There are some students of history who claim that certain *kami* were personified objects or phenomena which later came to be regarded as ancestors, and others who claim that they were actually ancestors who became posthumously identified with deified objects or phenomena. Some even claim, for instance, that the Sun Goddess [Amaterasu] was actually an ancestress who was deified and identified with the sun. It is certain, however, that, until the introduction of Chinese civilization, ancestor worship was extremely vague and unsystematized.

Since the early Japanese lived in an agricultural society, interest in fertility and food production was dominant. Prominent among the deities worshipped were the goddess of food, the god of grains, and other deities, such as the storm god, who directly affected the welfare of the people through their connection with food production. The personification of the sun was in part an expression of this interest. Phallicism, one phase of the idea of fertility, was very prevalent. And the most important festivals were those related to harvests.

The one essential for approaching the deities was purification. Disease, wounds, death, sexual intercourse, and menstruation were regarded as defilements. Before participating in any Shinto ritual, the worshipper would not only cleanse himself physically but would also seek to purify such pollutions. There was no sense of moral guilt or sin in Shinto. All that was required was ceremonial purification in the presence of the deities. This purification was accomplished by various magical rites, which still provide the basis for the many purification rituals to be found in modern Shinto.

Forms of Worship

The worshipper in prehistoric antiquity usually faced the object of devotion itself, which might be a tree, stone, mountain, or sunrise. He performed his devotions standing within a sacred enclosure, which was often set within a quiet grove. In time, a shrine was erected at the spot, or, if the object of worship was a distant mountain,

A torii stands at the entrance to a forest shrine.

only a covering was prepared under which the worshipper might stand. The shrines were always of extremely simple construction with no decorative effects, usually nothing more than a thatched roof supported by straight pillars. Within there would be a symbolic representation of deity, a substitute spirit which might be a stone, a mirror, or some other symbol of divinity. There were no images in ancient Shinto. Around the precincts could be found straw ropes from which were suspended small strips of paper. These marked off the sacred spot and were to protect the objects of worship from evil influences. And inside the shrines there were small wands or short sticks with hemp or paper strips inserted at one end. These were symbolic offerings and occasionally were regarded as symbols of divinity. At the entrance to the shrine compound, there stood a *torii*, a symbolic gateway dividing the sacred from the secular. Somewhere near the shrine, there would be fresh water, a spring or a basin, for the purification of the worshippers.

Along with simple nature and spirit worship, there was the worship of clan deities. These tutelary [guardian] deities were those which were believed to be the particular benefactors of each community or which in some cases were thought to be the progenitors of the clans. The common beliefs and traditions of the clans were based on these clan cults. The family head was both father and chief priest. In time, there developed the practice of revering ancestral or tutelary deities. The ascendancy of the Yamato clan [ca. fourth century] raised its clan deity, the Sun Goddess, to the position of ancestress of all other clans. While she achieved this position of grandeur and her qualities became more clearly defined, she also became more remote, and local deities took on a deeper meaning by sharing in her reflected glory.

On the one hand, there had developed a religious system devoted to nature deities of more or less local interest; on the other hand, there had come into being a national cult centering in the Sun Goddess, who was regarded as the guardian of agriculture and the ancestress of the ruling family. Due to the lack of historical texts prior to the seventh and eighth centuries, it is almost impossible to tell the exact nature of the Sun Goddess cult before it was subjected to foreign influences. Without doubt, the compilers of the first historical narratives colored their accounts and, in some cases, added ideas and traditions not indigenous to Japan. The *Kojiki* (Chronicle of Ancient Events) and the *Nihongi* (Chronicles of Japan) were the first scriptures of Shinto, and the religious ideas they present have persisted to modern times. The cycle of cosmological myths centering in three creative deities, who are said to have come from primeval chaos, are Chinese in origin and played very little part in Shinto festivals. The trinity consists of a central deity, the Heavenly-Central-Lord (Ame-no-minakanushi) and two subordinates, the High-Producing (Takami-musubi) and the Divine-Producing (Kami-musubi), who appear to represent the male and female principles. These three deities of creation gradually disappeared in Shinto worship, as did a succession of similar deities, but they reappeared in the Tokugawa period [1600–1668] and are indicative of a monotheistic or at least henotheistic [worship of one god out of several] tendency in Shinto.

The last of the succession of deities mentioned above were the Male-Who-Invites (Izanagi) and the Female-Who-Invites (Izanami). These produced the terrestrial world and gave birth to wind, water, mists, food, mountains, and other natural phenomena which also became deities. The ideas of spontaneous and sexual generation exist side by side in Japanese mythology with complete naivete. The final offspring of this divine couple were the Heavenly-Shining-Goddess (Amaterasu Omikami), the Moon-Ruler (Tsuki-yomi), and the Valiant-Swift-Impetuous-Hero (Takehaya-susanowo). The Sun Goddess ruled the realm of light, including heaven and earth; the Moon God ruled the night; and the Valiant-Swift-Impetuous-Hero ruled the mysterious nether regions.

The Sun Goddess became the progenitrix [matriarch] of a line of lesser deities who, according to the official myth, ruled the world. As the ancestress of Emperor Jimmu, ruler of the conquering Yamato clan, she dominated all other clan deities and came to be worshipped as the progenitrix of the entire race. The three insignia of the imperial throne—a mirror, a sword, and a jewel—were legendary gifts from her to the Yamato rulers. As the supreme deity of Shinto, her worship has occasionally given impetus to monotheistic trends in Shinto.

Shinto Mythology Reflects the Japanese Landscape

by Juliet Piggott

In the following selection Juliet Piggott summarizes some of the earliest written myths of Shinto. Unlike the other major world religions, Shinto has no body of sacred texts describing basic beliefs or rituals, and it has no founders or prophets. Instead, it has evolved as Japanese culture has, a process that continues today. Nevertheless, Shintoists have come to believe in a prehistoric Age of the Gods during which the founding deities emerged and the Japanese islands were created.

Piggott's main source for her myths is one of the first written Japanese chronicles, the *Nihongi*, or *Nihon shoki*, written using Chinese characters in A.D. 720. It divides the Shinto deities, or *kami*, into two categories, heavenly and earthly. Piggott's stories are of both, and she shows that even heavenly *kami* such as the sun goddess Amaterasu and the storm god Susano had vibrant personalities and human characteristics. Throughout, Piggot emphasizes the fact that these stories are closely connected to the Japanese landscape and to natural forces, as the story of two earthly *kami*, Fire Fade and Fire Flash, makes clear. Juliet Piggott's father and grandfather both worked in an official capacity for the Japanese government in the late 1800s and early 1900s. Her other books include *Fairy Tales of Japan.*

Izanagi and Izanami

Out of the primeval oily ocean mass, a reed-like substance emerged. This became a deity, and at the same time two other divine creatures, male and female, came into being. Little is told of this original trio, but they did produce generations of gods and goddesses in their celestial land, and after a period of unmeasured time a pair of gods were finally created called Izanagi and Izanami. Their names in translation are 'Male-who-invites' and 'Female-who-invites' respectively. They came down from their heaven to the oily mass by a bridge, generally accepted to have been a rainbow. Izanagi disturbed the primeval ocean with his spear and the drops from its tip congealed and, in falling, formed the island of Ono-koro or 'self-coagulating.' This is one of the earliest suggestions of phallicism in Japanese mythology.

Although Izanagi and Izanami were supposedly brother and sister, they married on Ono-koro. They learned the art of love-making by watching a pair of wagtails, and these water birds are still associated with the couple. Even the god of Scarecrows cannot frighten wagtails, a blessing given the birds at their creation.

Among the offspring of Izanagi and Izanami were geographical landmarks, including the rest of the Japanese islands, waterfalls, and mountains, trees, herbs and the wind. The wind completed the creation of Japan, for he it was who blew away the hazy mists and revealed the scattered islands for the first time. The first child of the two gods was miscarried (supposedly through a misdemeanour on Izanami's part at the marriage ceremony) and this jellyfish-like creature was, not surprisingly, put into the sea.

All their other children survived. The last to be born after the string of islands had been formed and populated was the cause of his mother's death. He was the god of fire. After his birth, Izanami became ill with a burning fever which finally killed her. She went to the Underworld—Yomi, the Land of Gloom—but Izanagi followed her there in spite of her protests. She chased him, aided by hideous female spirits, in order to punish him for pursuing her, but he just managed to escape back to the world. At the entrance of Yomi, she screamed after him that in revenge she would denude the world of its inhabitants by destroying a thousand daily. However, Izanagi replied that he would create fifteen hundred each day.

In this story not only did the pair, through their marriage and progeny, establish the pattern of nature for all time, but through their 'divorce' they created mortal life and death.

Izanagi kept his word, and after undergoing a ritual purification to wash away the effects of his descent into the Underworld, he gave birth to the Sun goddess, the Moon god and to Susano the Storm god. In one version, it is told that these three were created from Izanagi's eyes.

Amaterasu, the Sun Goddess

Many myths explain natural phenomena. The Sun and Moon brother and sister have an uneasy relationship and sit in their celestial land which is curiously like Japan in structure, with their backs to one another:

hence day and night. The Sun goddess, Amaterasu, is looked upon as the deity from whom the imperial family is descended. Of the host of stories connected with her, one of the best known is that of her withdrawal into a cave. Amaterasu and Susano were not friends. As the Storm God, he was a troublesome character. He once visited her domain on the pretext of making amends for previous unruly behaviour. Instead he destroyed her rice fields by loosing piebald colts among them and generally desecrated much of her property. She retaliated by retiring into a cave, thus darkening the whole world. Amaterasu did not come out until a goddess, encouraged by a multitude of minor gods and goddesses, all making a great uproar the while, performed a dance which some describe as merry and others as obscene, outside the cave. Overcome by curiosity, Amaterasu emerged and in doing so saw her reflection in a mirror which the gods had fashioned and hung on a tree while she was in hiding. This was the first mirror and it forms a part of the imperial regalia of Japan. Since the cave episode, the world has experienced normal day and night.

Susano, the Storm God

Susano, however, is not entirely limited to his role as Storm god. His name has been translated as 'Swift-Impetuous-Deity' and 'The Impetuous Male.' He was banished from Amaterasu's celestial country and went to the Province of Izumo on the coast of the Sea of Japan in Honshu. From there be was said to have planted forests on the coasts of Korea from the hairs of his beard, and because of this he is associated with forests in general. He is depicted as being heavily bearded and is perhaps connected with the hairy Ainu [an indigenous people who now inhabit Japan's far north].

Susano and his progeny are also associated with Izumo. His grandson, Omi-tsu-nu, on coming into his inheritance, wanted to extend the territory of the province. He changed the coastline to its present shape by dragging towards him pieces of land from Korea and also certain islands off the Izumo coast by means of ropes connected to a mountain. These portions of land, when all joined together, formed the peninsula in the north of Izumo. The last rope used in this complicated operation was tied to Mt Taisen, and Yomi beach, which lies at its foot, is said to be the remains of it.

Many other stories are told about Susano in good or evil guise. One of the most popular tells how he killed an eight-headed dragon in Izumo. He did this by making it drunk with eight bowls of *sake*, the Japanese alcoholic drink made from distilled rice. In one version the sake is poisoned. Susano used his courage and cunning to kill the dragon in order to rescue a minor goddess, a girl, whose many sisters had been eaten in turn annually by the dragon. The heroine in the story was the last surviving daughter of the family and as could be expected, she married Susano. Their children pass into mythical history and beyond.

In the tail of the dead dragon, Susano found the sword which is another part of the imperial regalia. During one of the infrequent periods when he and his sister were amiably disposed towards one another he gave it to Amaterasu. In return she gave him some of her jewels, which form the third part of the regalia. On another occasion she gave him other jewels which he used as hail and lightning in his capacity of Storm god.

Izumo province provides the setting for most of the earliest myths, but other parts of Japan have theirs too.

One such myth explains why there are no foxes on the island of Shikoku. After the time of the Buddhist saint Kobo Daishi (774–835 A.D.), no story set there has a fox in it, for he was supposed to have purged the island of the animals by driving them into the sea. The animal stories of Shikoku have badgers, cats or dogs in place of the mischievous or evil fox.

Trees and Rocks

All over Japan one hears stories of trees which have a peculiar or beautiful shape. One pair of twisted and entwined pines is supposed to be a pair of lovers. The boy and girl wandered far from their village and as night fell, were afraid to return and face either the displeasure of their families or the taunts of their friends. All night they embraced and talked of their love, and when morning broke they had been transformed into these pine trees. Another pair of pines is said to be a devoted couple who died at the same time. These trees represent fidelity as well as the more usual prosperous old age.

In Kyushu on the coast of Matsura there is a rock known as the Rock of Sayo-hime. Like so many curiously shaped rock formations, it has its story. Sayo-hime was the wife of an official whose duties took him to China. In ancient times Matsura was the port for the Asian mainland. She stood waving him good-bye long after his ship had disappeared, until eventually her body turned into the rock bearing her name.

Uke-Mochi

Just as the physical formation of the volcanic islands provide stories or myths, so do their crops. The Moon god was sent down to Earth by his elder sister, Amaterasu, to see that the Food deity, Uke-mochi, was performing her duties. In order to entertain this higher being, since Amaterasu and her two brothers took precedence over other deities, Uke-mochi opened her mouth while facing the fields and boiled rice streamed from it. When she faced the sea, fish and edible seaweed were regurgitated, and when she faced the wooded hills, game of various kinds came forth. The Moon god was, understandably, unappreciative of the manner in which the repast was served, and so violent was his anger that he killed the unfortunate Uke-mochi. However, even in death her body continued its work, for cows and horses emerged from her head, silkworms from her eyebrows, millet grew from her forehead and a rice plant sprang from her stomach. The earliest record tells the story as pertaining to Susano but a slightly later one, the *Nihongi*, makes the Moon god the murderer of Uke-mochi.

Fire Fade and Fire Flash

Physical and climatic phenomena, such as tides and hurricanes, also play a large part in Japanese mythology. Earthquakes, too, are an integral and hazardous part of life in Japan. There were two mythical princes about whom a well known story is told. Their names vary from version to version, and so to avoid confusion, the English names—Fire Fade and Fire Flash—are used here. This tale appears in different forms in the most ancient annals of all. Fire Fade was the younger of the two brothers, and an excellent hunter. Fire Flash was a fine fisherman. They had a competition in order to see if each could excel at the other's sport. Fire Fade not only caught nothing, but lost Fire Flash's fish hook. The elder brother ordered Fire Fade to find the hook. This seemingly impossible task was accomplished in a series of adventures. The Old Man of the Sea advised Fire Fade to sail out to sea in a little boat. This he did and met and fell in love with the Sea King's daughter. In due time they married and found the missing fish hook in the throat of a *tai* or sea bream. Homesickness for Japan (a recurrent mythological theme and still a national characteristic), coupled with the duty of returning the fish hook to Fire Flash, made Fire Fade return to land. His wife, pregnant at the time, gave him the Tide Ebbing Jewel and the Tide Flowing Jewel. These Jewels of the Sea reappear in myths at intervals, being used for various purposes.

The Hira Hurricane

The hurricane around Lake Biwa [Japan's largest freshwater lake, about three hundred miles west of Tokyo] which often happens in August is called the Hira Hurricane, for it blows from the Hira mountain range. A legend concerning it tells of a young girl who lived on the lakeside and became infatuated with the lighthouse keeper on the other side of the lake. She used to visit him, crossing the water at night guided by the light he kept flashing across the lake. All went well for a time. But her indifference to the dangers of drowning as well as her wanton behaviour suddenly made the lighthouse keeper wonder if perhaps she were an evil enchantress and not just an attractive, brave young woman ready to visit her lover nightly in spite of a perilous voyage. So one night, in order to test his theory, he put out the light. She got lost on the darkened lake and finally, in fear and rage at the lighthouse keeper for failing to help her reach him, flung herself from her boat. As she drowned she cursed him and his lighthouse. A hurricane blew up at once and did not subside until both the lighthouse and its keeper were no more.

The Cherry and the Plum

The Japanese love flowers and the indigenous plants of Japan have their myths. Sir Francis Piggott [the author's father and founder of the Japan Society of London] wrote in his *The Garden of Japan:* One day Kinto Fujiwara, Great Advisor of State, disputed with the Minister of Uji which was the fairest of spring and autumn flowers. Said the Minister: "The Cherry is surely best among the flowers of spring, the Chrysanthemum among those of autumn." Then Kinto said, "How can the Cherry-blossom be the best? You have forgotten the Plum." Their dispute came at length to be confined to the superiority of the Cherry and Plum, and of other flowers little notice was taken. At length Kinto, not wishing to offend the Minister, did not argue so vehemently as before, but said, "Well, have it so: the Cherry may be the prettier of the two; but when once you have seen the red Plum-blossom in the snow at the dawn of a spring morning, you will no longer forget its beauty." This truly was a gentle saying.

In such a setting, mythological stories about flowers and plants abound. One concerns two grasses, Patrinia and Miscanthus. They often grow near each other, and a story gives the reason for this. A girl, abandoned by her lover, drowned herself. After her body had been recovered and she had been buried, Patrinia grew from her grave. Later, in remorse for having driven his mistress to suicide, the man too drowned himself—in the same river. He was buried beside her, and from his grave grew Miscanthus.

A small leafed ivy, growing in rocky places, is called *Teika-kazura*. Teika was a thirteenth century poet who loved a poetess, who also happened to be a princess. After her death she was buried near a Buddhist monastery in Saga. In his grief Teika clung to the tomb and his desolation is perpetuated in the ivy which grows all over it.

Ninigi and the Blossom Princess

Although short life was not always the pattern, there was a time when the princes of the imperial house were not blessed with old age. Perhaps this gave rise to the myth that when Amaterasu's grandson, Ninigi, was sent to Japan with the three items of the imperial regalia, he fell in love with Ko-no-hana, the Princess who makes the Flowers of the Trees to Blossom. Her father, Oho-yama, the Great Mountain Possessor, had an elder daughter, Iha-naga, Princess Long-as-the-Rocks. Ninigi was given the choice of either daughter. He remained faithful to the Blossom Princess and married her. The elder sister, who had wanted to marry the 'Beloved Grandson' herself, was deeply hurt by the marriage and stated that had Ninigi married her, their offspring would have lived long—as long as do the rocks. But now her nephews would bloom and fade and fall as the blossoms in the spring. In spite of this dire prophecy, the children of Ninigi and his chosen bride included Fire Flash and Fire Fade, the latter becoming the grandfather of the first emperor of Japan, Jimmu Tenno, through his marriage to the daughter of the Sea King.

After the Sea King's daughter had followed Fire Fade

Blossoms cover a cherry tree in Kyoto. The cherry blossom has deep significance in Japanese culture.

back to earth and he had returned the fish hook to his elder brother, she asked him to build her a shelter in which she could give birth to the expected child. She went into this hut as her labour began and commanded him not to watch the delivery. Fire Fade did look and to his horror saw that she had taken on the form of a dragon for her confinement. He fled from the place of her labour, but on his return found a mortal boy child in the small building: his wife had returned to her Sea King father for good, having been seen on land in her dragon shape. She sent her sister from the sea to look after the baby and when he reached manhood he married this aunt. Their child was the first emperor.

Whatever the general life span of the princes of the imperial family may have been, a grove of cherry trees surrounds the shrine to the consort of Ninigi, and her father and sister are venerated as Father Mountain and the Rock Princess.

The crest of the imperial army was a single cherry

blossom, symbolising the glorious if short life of one dedicated to duty. Bamboo has long been a lucky symbol, representing tenacity and courage. The bamboo will bend in the wind but not break. It is a plant which grows profusely in the country and is admired for its grace as well as for its symbolic meaning. It is used both at festivals for ornamentation and in varying forms as a crest. Flowers play a far more important part in the heraldry of Japan than in other countries. It is the flora rather than the fauna which predominates in the crests of the old families.

Their gardens show how aware of the beauty of their countryside are the Japanese. Mountains, deep valleys, terraced fields, waterfalls, streams and rock formations all find their place in these often small but accurately proportioned gardens. They are landscapes in miniature. The plant life and the land in which it grows are as peculiarly Japanese as the myths surrounding them.

The Sun Goddess Amaterasu and the Storm God Susano Quarrel

by Anonymous

In this selection from "The Age of the Gods," the early portion of the *Nihongi*, or *Nihon shoki*, one of the earliest chronicles of Japan written in the early eighth century, the anonymous authors recite a story concerning two of the earliest and most central Shinto deities, or *kami:* Amaterasu and Susano, who are both referred to by their far-longer full names. Even though Amaterasu has already settled in the heavens, she still faces the approach of her impetuous and irresponsible brother, Susano, whose intentions are unclear. She prepares for a conflict but finds that Susano merely wants to see her before he departs for the "Nether Land." The two agree to seal their relationship by producing new *kami* who serve as the founders of some of Japan's important aristocratic families. One effect of such stories was clearly to try to establish the divine origins of Japan's early elite groups.

Now at first when Sosa no wo no Mikoto [also known as Susano] went up to Heaven, by reason of the fierce-

Anonymous, *Nihongi, Chronicles of Japan from the Earliest Times to* A.D. *697*, trans. W.G. Aston. London: George Allen & Unwin Ltd., 1896.

ness of his divine nature there was a commotion in the sea, and the hills and mountains groaned aloud. Ama-terasu no Oho-kami, knowing the violence and wickedness of this Deity, was startled and changed countenance, when she heard the manner of his coming. She said (to herself):—"Is my younger brother coming with good intentions? I think it must be his purpose to rob me of my kingdom. By the charge which our parents gave to their children, each of us has his own allotted limits. Why, therefore, does he reject the kingdom to which he should proceed, and make bold to come spying here?" So she bound up her hair into knots and tied up her skirts into the form of trousers. Then she took an august string of five hundred Yasaka jewels, which she entwined around her hair and wrists. Moreover, on her back she slung a thousand-arrow quiver and a five-hundred-arrow quiver. On her lower arm she drew a dread loud-sounding elbow-pad. Brandishing her bow end upwards, she firmly grasped her sword-hilt, and stamping on the hard earth of the courtyard, sank her thighs into it as if it had been foam-snow, and kicked it in all directions. Having thus put forth her dread manly valour, she uttered a mighty cry of defiance, and questioned him in a straightforward manner. Sosa no wo no Mikoto answered and said:—"From the beginning my heart has not been black. But as in obedience to the stern behest of our parents, I am about to proceed for ever to the Nether Land, how could I bear to depart without having seen face to face thee my elder sister? It is for this reason that I have traversed on foot the clouds and mists and have come hither from afar. I am surprised that my elder sister should, on the contrary, put on so stern a countenance."

Then Ama-terasu no Oho-kami again asked him, saying:—"If this be so, how wilt thou make evident the redness of thy heart?" He answered and said:—"Let us, I pray thee, make an oath together. While bound by this oath, we shall surely produce children. If the children which I produce are females, then it may be taken that I have an impure heart. But if the children are males, then it must be considered that my heart is pure."

Upon this Ama-terasu no Oho-kami asked for Sosa no wo no Mikoto's ten-span sword, which she broke into three pieces, and rinsed in the true-well of Heaven. Then chewing them with a crunching noise, she blew them away, and from the true-mist of her breath Gods were born. The first was named Ta-gori-bime, the next Tagi-tsu-bime, and the next Chiki-shima-bime, three daughters in all.

After this Sosa no wo no Mikoto begged from Ama-terasu no Oho-kami the august string of 500 Yasaka jewels which was entwined in her hair and round her wrists, and rinsed it in the true-well of Heaven. Then chewing it with a crunching noise, he blew it away, and from the true-mist of his breath there were Gods produced. The first was called Masa-ya-a-katsu-kachi-hayabi-ama no oshi-no-mimi no Mikoto, and the next Ama no ho-hi no Mikoto. This is the ancestor of the Idzumo no Omi, and of the Hashi no Muraji. The next was Ama-tsu hiko-ne no Mikoto. He was the ancestor of the Ohoshi-kafuchi no Atahe, and of the Yamashiro no Atahe. The next was Iku-tsu-hiko-ne no Mikoto, and the next Kumano no kusu-bi no Mikoto—in all five males [by "ancestor of" is meant the founder of Japan's aristocratic clans].

Then Ama-terasu no Oho-kami said:—"Their seed was in the beginning the august necklace of 500 Yasaka jewels which belonged to me. Therefore these five male

Deities are all my children." So she took these children and brought them up. Moreover she said:—"The ten-span sword belonged to thee, Sosa no wo no Mikoto. Therefore these three female Deities are all thy children." So she delivered them to Sosa no wo no Mikoto. These are the deities which are worshipped by the Munagata no Kimi of Tsukushi [lords of Kyushu].

Sacred Space, Sacred Time, and the Vital Force

by Kodansha International

The following selection examines Shinto in practice. The authors, contributors to a book on both historical and modern Japan, assert that Shinto denotes both sacred space and sacred time. The sacred space is where the *kami*, or gods, can be called upon and does not necessarily have to be a fully constructed shrine but might offer only hints of walls and borders. Sacred time places the origins of the *kami*, and of Japan itself, within the flow of history and also organizes the yearly calendar of rituals and festivals. The essence of Shinto worship, meanwhile, is the calling up of the vital force, or *tama*, which animates all life and might be found, during worship ceremonies, in various sacred objects.

Shinto practice is circumscribed within the context of sacred space and sacred time. The oldest known form of sacred space is a rectangular area covered with pebbles, surrounded by stones, and marked off by a rope linking four corner pillars; in the middle of this area is a stone (*iwasaki* or *iwakura*), a pillar, or a tree (*himorogi*). This ritually purified place where divinities were invoked (kanjo) was located in the midst of a sacred grove. The typical shrine (jinja) is located near the source of a river at the foot of a mountain. Surrounded by a fence (tamagaki), its entrance is marked by a wooden gate (torii) of simple style, on which a rope (shimenawa) has been fixed.

The etymology [origin] of the term kami, which is often rendered as "deity" or "god" but is translated here as "divinity," is unclear. The Shinto pantheon, which is structured only at the level of the imperial tradition, consists of the yaoyorozu no kami (literally, "800 myriads of divinities"). Therefore, the presence of the kami is overwhelming and pervades all aspects of life. Natural phenomena—wind, sun, moon, water, mountains, trees—are kami. Specialized kami overlook and patronize human activities and even dwell in man-made objects. Certain kami are divinized ancestors or great figures of the past, and until 1945 the emperor was regarded as divine.

Each kami is endowed with an efficient force called tama, which is the object of religious activity and may be seen as violent (aramitama) or peaceful (nigimitama). Tama, the force that supports all life, dwells in human beings as tamashii and departs at the time of death. The tama of a kami is called upon at the outset of a ceremony to listen to the praise of the community and to its wishes. It is then offered food, praised again, and sent back. During ceremonies the tama of a divinity is thought to invest itself in the sacred tree or stone described above, or, more commonly, in a stone, root, branch, sword, mirror, or other object that is kept out of sight in a shrine. As the tama is inexhaustible, it may be invoked at many different locations.

Sacred time is that of the myths of the origin of the

gods and of the land, as well as the time during which these origins are commemorated. Rituals and ceremonies are performed at each shrine by priests or by a rotating group of community members, on a cyclical and yearly basis. Each word uttered, each gesture and movement, and each ceremony is prescribed in ritual codes that are today set for all shrines in the *Saishi kitei*, published by the National Organization of Shrines (Jinja Honcho).

Two Types of Ritual Purification

The other central aspect of Shinto ritual is purification. Grounded in mythology, it takes two forms: *misogi*, purification from contact with sullying elements (*kegare*) such as disease or death, and *harae*, the restoration of proper relationships after wrongdoing, through the offering of compensation. Misogi is held to have originated in the myth of the deity Izanagi no Mikoto, who, having followed his consort Izanami no Mikoto to the Land of Darkness (Yomi no Kuni; the netherworld) and seen her in a state of decomposition, returns to the world and cleanses himself in a stream. As he does so, the purification of his left eye results in the birth of the solar divinity Amaterasu Omikami, the purification of his right eye results in the appearance of the lunar divinity Tsukuyomi no Mikoto, and the purification of his nose causes the appearance of the storm divinity Susanoo no Mikoto.

The second form of purification, harae, is held to derive from the myth of Susanoo no Mikoto, who, after rampaging through the palace of his sister Amaterasu, is compelled to make recompense by offering up a great quantity of goods and having his beard cut and nails

A man sips water to purify himself before entering the grounds of a Shinto shrine.

pulled off. Ritual implements, such as the folded paper strips (*shide*) that are affixed to ropes, gates, and sacred trees, and offerings of hemp, ramie, salt, and rice derive from the tradition of harae and serve the function of misogi; hence the origin of the general term misogi harae for purificatory practices. The emphasis on purity in Shinto worship is also manifested in the custom of undergoing a period of interdiction (*imi* or *kessai*) of as long as 30 days, which requires avoidance of contact with death, disease, menstruating women, and disfigured persons and abstention from sexual activity and the eating of meat, as well as adherence to conventions in food preparation, clothing, and bathing.

Shinto Evolves into an Organized Religion

by H. Byron Earhart

In the following selection, scholar of religion H. Byron Earhart examines the nature and forms of organized Shinto in early Japan. Shinto had evolved out of some of the beliefs and customs of prehistoric Japanese people, and, as Earhart implies, elements of these beliefs and customs continued as Shinto became more organized. This took place primarily in the first half of the Heian period of Japanese history lasting from 794–1185. During these years, when the capital of Japan was the city of Kyoto and court aristocrats developed a highly sophisticated and refined culture, numerous important developments took place. Shinto rituals conducted by priests were solidified, the model for the construction and layout of Shinto shrines was established, and a Shinto calendar of holidays emerged. The calendar, as Earhart points out, reflected the rhythms of life in an agricultural society and also commemorated important events in national life, such as the enshrinement of a new emperor.

During the centuries of the Heian era, Japan was also absorbing such newer outside influences as Chinese culture and Buddhism. Earhart closes this selection by citing a scholar, Tsunetsugu Muraoka, who describes ways in which Shinto, despite its integration with these other influences, remained a distinct way of thought and life. H. Byron Earhart taught religion at Western Michigan University and was the author of such books as *Religions in the Japanese Experience* and *A Religious Study of the Mount Haguro Sect of Shugendo.*

In Japan as in many early civilizations, religion and the priesthood served as arms of the government: The emperor (as the divine ruler) was responsible for the ritual as well as the administrative propriety of the realm. In many ancient traditions, the perpetuation of the ritual order was necessary for maintaining the whole cosmic order. Therefore, it is important to note the contents of this ritual.

From Yayoi times [ca. 250 B.C. to A.D. 250] to the present, Japanese religion, especially Shinto ceremonies, has been linked with every phase of growing rice. Although the planting of rice occasions a festival, this and other phases are overshadowed by the climax of the rice harvest, at which time the new rice is offered up to the *kami* [gods] as thanksgiving. Even the enthronement ceremony for a new emperor was patterned after the annual thanksgiving harvest ceremony. Other important annual ceremonies are the public purifications that take place at the midpoint and end of the year.

The ritual prayers (*norito*) for the public ceremonies are recorded in codes called the *Engishiki*. The *Engishiki*, or Codes of the Engi Era [901–922], were not written down until 927, but they contain materials that predate this era. In particular the *norito* or liturgies presented in Shinto ceremonies, recorded in the *Engishiki*, are extremely valuable for understanding early Shinto. The priest who read the *norito* served as an intermediary between humans and the *kami*. Usually the priest "called down" the *kami* at the beginning of the ceremony and "sent them away" at the close of the ceremony. Sometimes this was acted out by opening and closing the doors to the inner sanctum (*shinden* or "*kami* hall") housing the sacred object (*shintai* or "*kami* body"), which symbolized the presence of the enshrined *kami*.

The Shinto Shrine

The rites and celebrations of Shinto center on shrines (*jinja*), which are still found in the smallest villages as well as in the largest cities. (In English usage the word "shrine" is the general term for the Shinto building—*jinja* or *miya;* the word "temple" is the general term for the Buddhist building—*tera* or *-ji*.) Normally one passes through a sacred arch (*torii*), which helps define the sacred precincts of the shrine. Devout believers purify themselves by pouring water on their hands and rinsing their mouths. The present shrine buildings betray Buddhist and Chinese architectural influence, but some are still built according to the ancient models. These shrines are built on poles above the ground and have a thatched roof. They can be seen today at Ise, one of the Shinto strongholds that consciously attempted to reject Buddhist influence. (At Ise, the Sun Goddess, Amaterasu, is enshrined.) This ancient shrine architecture seems to have affinities with architecture to the south of Japan. As Shinto scholars like to point out, its natural beauty is accentuated by the use of wood and thatch left bare of decorations.

One theory concerning ancient Japanese religion is

that originally there were no shrine buildings; rather, a shrine was simply a sacred precinct set apart in a certain area or around a sacred object such as a tree or a stone. Sacred precincts often were the sites where the ancestral spirits dwelled. This is a valuable insight for linking ancestor worship with Japanese notions of *kami* and festivals. Only later did there come to appear the twofold Shinto architecture, with a worship hall *(haiden)* in front and a smaller *kami* hall in back. The worship hall is where the priests (and sometimes the people) directed prayers toward the *kami* hall, which contained the presence of the enshrined *kami* symbolized by a sacred object such as a mirror or sword. As Shinto became organized in medieval times, local shrines were considered to enshrine specific *kami* named in the *Kojiki* [an early text concerned partially with Shinto].

Religious activities at the Shinto shrine took place in terms of the rhythm of the religious year and an individual's life span. The earlier Japanese religious tradition seems to have observed the rhythm of the year, with spring festivals and fall festivals to mark the planting and harvesting of rice. Even today, the spring and fall festivals are still important celebrations in most city shrines. Of great importance, too, have been the purification ceremonies at midyear and New Year's, to wash away the physical and spiritual "pollutions" or "defilements" of the previous half-year.

Seasonal Festivals

Five traditional festivals (also revealing Chinese influence) have come to be celebrated throughout Japan: (1) first day of the first month, New Year's festival; (2) third day of the third month, the girls' festival (or dolls' festival); (3) fifth day of the fifth month, boys' festival; (4) seventh day of the seventh month, star festival; (5) ninth day of the ninth month, chrysanthemum festival. Although this formal system of five festivals is a complex mixture of Chinese and Japanese elements, the festivals have become inseparable from Japanese home and village life.

Religious activities at the shrine also revolved around the events in an individual's life. Traditionally, the newborn child was dedicated at a shrine on his or her first trip out of the house. At other specific ages a child visited the shrines again. Usually special youth groups helped carry out the processions of festivals. In more recent times it has become the custom to be married in a shrine. A visit to a shrine has always been appropriate in any time of crisis. For example, a soldier going off to war would pray for safekeeping at his local (guardian) shrine where he had been carried as a baby. All such visits brought individuals into contact with the *kami*, the sacred power that sustains human life.

Distinctive Characteristics of Shinto

The preceding discussion of the history and nature of Shinto shows how native and foreign elements were blended together into one great national tradition. At the same time the discussion shows that it is a mistake to view Shinto simply as the indigenous religion of Japan by falsely contrasting all other traditions as foreign. Nevertheless, many secondary Western interpretations of Shinto have perpetuated these misleading notions. Misconceptions arose partly because Western scholars tried too hard to compartmentalize Shinto and Buddhism into separate religions. Also, the emphatically national character of Shinto was overexaggerated by Western scholars who studied Shinto during its nationalistic phase from about 1867 to 1945. It is now time for a reevaluation of Shinto in more balanced terms. . . .

Because Shinto has such a long history and has interacted so much with other traditions, it is difficult to distinguish Shinto sharply from all other Japanese traditions. But Tsunetsugu Muraoka, a Japanese scholar widely respected for his critical interpretations of Shinto history, claims that there are three distinctive characteristics of Shinto. First, there is Shinto's emphasis on the identity of the Japanese nation with the imperial family and the descent of this family from ancestral *kami*. Second, Shinto practices a "realistic" affirmation of life and values in this world, accepting life and death, good and evil, as inevitable parts of the world we live in. Third, Shinto features a reverence for the "bright" and "pure" in all matter and thought, attempting to overcome physical pollution with rites of exorcism and bad thoughts with a "pure and bright heart." In Muraoka's interpretation of Shinto and its distinctive features, the first characteristic is political, the second is philosophical, and the third is ethical. The three are interrelated and interact to form the "intellectual strain" that defines Shinto throughout Japanese history. This interpretation is valuable because it locates *distinctive* characteristics of Shinto without claiming that they are the *unique* property of Shinto.

A Shinto Ritual for Good Harvests

by Anonymous

The following selection is a description of how Shinto priests were to conduct the ritual portion of the Toshigoi festival, a springtime celebration intended to ensure a rich agricultural year. It comes from the *Engishiki*, the first written collection of Shinto rituals, which appeared in the early tenth century and commemorated the brief Engi era (901–922) of Japanese history. The selection is one of many *norito*, or ritual prayers, contained in the collection.

Throughout, Shinto priests are enjoined to praise and supplicate the many *kami*, or gods, who were associated with natural things. The selection also provides instructions on how to perform various rituals. These instructions apply not only to the priests but to "sacred maidens," or "shrine virgins" as some describe them: young, unmarried women who serve as shrine attendants. The climax of the ceremony is a prayer to Amaterasu, the sun goddess and central deity of Shinto.

---

[1] Oh ye assembled shrine chiefs and all ye priests, hearken unto what we say. (Shrine chiefs and all priests

Anonymous, *Engi-Shiki: Procedures of the Engi Era, Books VI–X*, trans. Felicial Gresstii Bock. Tokyo: Sophia University, 1972. Copyright © 1972 by Monumenta Nipponica. Reproduced by permission.

are to respond 'Ooh!' to this and to all succeeding pro-
nouncements.)

[2] Before the mighty ancestral gods and goddesses
who augustly reside in the Plain of High Heaven, before
the many *kami* [gods] enshrined in heaven and earth,
we raise our words of praise; and to the mighty *kami* we
make bold to say: In this second month of this year, the
beginning of the sowing of seed, with choice offerings
from the divine descendant at this moment of the ma-
jestic and brilliant dawning of the morning light, we
humbly raise our words of praise.

[3] Before the presence of the *kami* who govern the
crops we do humbly speak, praying that the mighty
kami may vouchsafe to us the late-ripening harvest of
grain with foam on the water up to the elbows and
muddy water up to the thighs as the rice is cultivated—
may it grow into countless bundles of long-eared grain,
of vigorous grain. If the mighty *kami* grant that it ripen,
the first-fruits of the grain, a thousand, yea, ten thousand ears shall be offered up to them. Let the offering
jars be filled to the brims, yea, let the full-bellied jars be
arrayed in rows; the liquid and the grain shall we offer
up with our words of praise. Of things that grow in the
broad meadows and moors—sweet herbs and bitter
herbs; of things that live in the blue sea-plain—those
wide of fin and narrow of fin, even unto the seaweeds
of the deep and seaweeds of the shore; and for divine
raiment—bright cloth, shining cloth, soft cloth, and
coarse cloth—all these we humbly offer up with our
words of praise.

Before the presence of the mighty *kami* of the crops
we prepare to offer a white horse, a white boar, a white
cock, and all manner and variety of things. These we
offer as choice offerings from the divine descendant,

with the words of praise which we humbly speak.

[4] Before the mighty *kami* to whom the great Sacred Maidens [female shrine attendants] offer words of praise, we humbly speak. We utter the hallowed names of Kami-musubi, Takami-musubi, Iku-musubi, Taru-musubi, Tamatsume-musubi, Oomiya-no-me, Oomiketsu-no-kami and Kotoshironushi, to all of whom we now offer our praises. May this age of the divine descendant of heaven be an everlasting age, as firm as solid rock, as unchanging as enduring rock. That it may flourish and be a happy reign, we present the choice offerings from the divine descendant to these mighty ancestral gods and goddesses as we offer up our words of praise.

[5] Before the presence of the mighty *kami* to whom the Igasuri Sacred Maidens raise their words of praise, we make bold to utter the hallowed names of Ikui, Sakui, Tsunagai, Asuha, and Haigi, and offer unto them our praises. By the command of the mighty *kami*, the columns of the divine palace are firmly set upon the bedrock beneath the land, and the crossed gable-boards reach up toward the Plain of High Heaven, as we humbly serve and worship at the sacred dwelling of the divine descendant. May it be sheltered from the gaze of heaven and from the blazing sun. Vouchsafe that from it the land in all directions may be governed and made a peaceful land, a tranquil land by the grace of the mighty *kami*. So we offer up the choice offerings from the divine descendant together with our words of praise.

[6] Before the presence of the mighty *kami* to whom the Mikado Sacred Maidens raise their words of praise, we make bold to utter the hallowed names of Kushi-iwamado-no-mikoto and Toyo-iwamado-no-mikoto and offer up to them our words of praise. May they defend with strength like a magic-working mound of rock

the august gates of the four directions; may they open the gates in the morning and close the gates in the evening. If things to be shunned come from below, let the *kami* protect below; if things to be shunned come from above, let the *kami* protect above. May they watch by night and watch by day we humbly pray, as with choice offerings of the divine descendant we offer up our words of praise.

[7] Before the presence of the mighty *kami* to whom the Ikushima Sacred Maidens raise their words of praise, we make bold to utter the hallowed names of Ikukuni and Tarukuni and offer up to them our words of praise. In all the many lands far and wide over which the mighty *kami* hold sway, to the uttermost corners whither creeping creatures may crawl, and as far as the salt foam of the flood tides reaches, may the narrow places be made wide and the steep places be made level, and may there be no escaping of waters in the lands far and wide. Let the mighty *kami* vouchsafe this to us, as with the choice offerings from the divine descendant of heaven we now raise our words of praise.

[8] And we turn now to the mighty presence of Amaterasu-ō-mikami who resides in Ise, making bold to say: In all the lands through which this mighty *kami* clearly sees, as far as the heavens stretch above and as far as the ground stretches beneath, to the uttermost heights of clouds in the blue, to the limits reached by the white clouds a-massing, to the uttermost reaches of the plain of the blue sea, on with pole and helm never dry the prows of ships do ply, yea, on the great ocean where sail heavy-laden ships and on the land routes where ropes are pulled taut over the loads of tribute cargo, may the mighty goddess vouchsafe to the divine descendant that treading over rough rocks and roots of

trees, as far as horses' hooves can travel, the narrow places may be made wide and the steep places made level, and may the distant countries send tribute pulled by dozens of hawsers [cables]. If the great ancestral goddess grant us this, before the presence of the great ancestral goddess we shall heap up our tribute of first-fruits like unto a range of hills, and if any be left over, may the divine descendant partake thereof. Moreover, may the reign of the divine descendant be an everlasting reign and may it be firm as hard rock, and enduring as solid rock, we pray. That it may flourish and be a happy reign, we humbly bow our necks way down like the cormorant in obeisance to the mighty ancestral gods and goddesses, and offer up the choice offerings from the divine descendant as we raise our words of praise.

[9] Before the presence of the mighty *kami* who dwell in the august districts we humbly speak. We make bold to utter the hallowed names of Takechi, Katsuragi, Toochi, Shiki, Yamanobe, and Sou. As we come humbly bearing the sweet herbs and the bitter herbs that grow in these six districts, may the *kami* vouchsafe that they provide food eternally for the divine descendants for with choice offerings from the divine descendant we raise our words of praise.

[10] Before the presence of the mighty *kami* that dwell in the openings of the mountains we humbly speak. Making bold to utter the sacred names of Asuka, Iware, Osaka, Hatsuse, Unebi, and Miminashi, we dare to cut the trunks and branches of great trees and small trees that sprout and grow in the farther mountains and the nearer mountains. And we come up bearing the wood therefrom that we may undertake to build a new and splendid august dwelling for the divine descendant, in which he may rest sheltered from the gaze

of heaven and from the blazing sun. May the *kami* vouchsafe that the land in all directions be calmed to a peaceful land. With choice offerings from the divine descendant of heaven we raise our words of praise.

[11] Before the presence of the water-dividing *kami* we humbly speak. We make bold to utter the sacred names of Yoshino, Uda, Tsuge, Katsuragi, as we humbly raise our words of praise. Let the mighty *kami* vouchsafe to us a crop of long-eared grain, of vigorous grain, in the late-ripening harvest of rice, and we shall offer up to the mighty *kami* the first-fruits in countless myriads of grains, the grain and the liquid made from it, filling the offering jars to the brims, and setting up the rows of full-bellied jars, we shall offer up our words of praise. If there be any left over, may it grace the table of the divine descendant for the august morning food and the august evening food, that he may partake of it for eternity. As in partaking his august cheeks become ruddy, so shall we bring the choice offerings from the divine descendant as we raise our words of praise, and let all those present hearken hereunto.

[12] We turn now and ask the Imbe, their frail shoulders bound with potent sleeve-ties [used to tie back sleeves when peforming religious duties] to consecrate the offerings that are here prepared, and ask the divine chiefs and all priests to humbly receive these offerings, and making no error, to bear them up and present them [to the *kami*].

CHAPTER 2

Shinto in Medieval and Early Modern Japan

Conflict and Compromise Between Buddhism and Shinto in Medieval Japan

by Michiko Yusa

Shinto is the oldest of the Japanese religions, but it is not the only religion. Many Japanese people practice Buddhism as well as Shinto, and they see no contradiction in adhering to two different faiths. Indeed, Japanese might practice aspects of Chinese-born Taoism and even Western Christianity as well as the other two faiths while living according to still another belief system, Confucianism, another Chinese import. Japan is a country of religious syncretism, or mixture.

Shinto and Buddhism, however, remain the main faiths, and Buddhism has historically presented the greatest challenge to Shinto. Of Indian origin, Buddhism arrived in Japan in the mid–sixth century by way of China and Korea. It was quickly adopted by Japanese elites, who associated the religion with the more sophisticated cultures of their neighbors. In the following selection scholar Michiko Yusa examines how Shinto and Buddhism became reconciled, mostly in the Heian era (794–1185). Perhaps the most important was how Shinto *kami*, or gods, came to be considered Buddhist bodhisattvas, or enlightened souls. In Buddhism the goal of believers is to achieve a state of enlightenment known as nirvana. Those who reach that goal become Buddhas, or awakened beings, unless they choose to remain among the living to help others achieve enlightenment. Those figures are bodhisattvas, or "little Buddhas." Also helping to reconcile the two faiths was the fact that believers tended to use Shinto when focused on worldly matters, and Buddhism when concerned with death or the afterlife. Michiko Yusa is professor of Japanese and East Asian studies at Western Washington University.

The relationship between Shinto and Buddhism has sometimes been cordial and other times antagonistic. From the mid–Heian period [794–1185] onward, however, these two traditions were to a large degree amalgamated—a phenomenon known as *shinbutsu shugo* (literally, "overlapping of Shinto and Buddhism"). No doubt this was in large part due to the fact that by this time the Tendai and Shingon [Buddhist] sects were firmly established, and had extended their reach to incorporate Shinto deities within their institutions.

The introduction of Buddhism into Japan was initially met with resistance . . . from those who adhered to Shinto; but Buddhism soon began to put down roots. During the Nara period [710–794], Shinto *kami* deities were considered to protect the Buddhist doctrines (*dharma*). For instance, the Shinto *kami* Hachiman, of the Usa Shrine in Kyushu [Japan's southernmost major island], was given the title of "Bodhisattva" (*Bosatsu*) in 746 for the support it had rendered to the successful completion of the construction of the great Buddhist temple of Todaiji, in Nara. Around this time, the *kami* worshipped by local powerful clans were woven into a Buddhist framework. According to the Indian Buddhist tradition, native Indian gods (*devas*) were considered not fully enlightened and were therefore subject to the law of karmic bondage, *samsara*. Residing in the world just one rung above human beings, the *devas* could fall down from heaven—in contrast to the perfectly enlightened sages and Buddhas, who enjoyed eternal bliss. Accordingly, a belief spread in Japan that the Shinto *kami* could improve their lot by taking refuge in Buddhism. "Shrine-temples," or *jinguji*, were erected on the precincts of Shinto shrines, so that the *kami* could undergo Buddhist practice and attain buddhahood. Extensive "conversion" of Shinto deities to Buddhism took place from the Nara to the early Heian period.

Both Saicho, the founder of the Tendai sect, and Kukai, the founder of the Shingon sect, accorded profound respect to the native *kami* spirits. Saicho took the ancient deity Ooyamagui as the protector god of Mt. Hiei and made the Hie Shrine (known as Hiyoshi Taisha today) in Sakamoto, on the eastern foothills of Mt. Hiei, the seat of this deity. (Mt. Hiei was in fact named after the Hie Shrine.) Likewise, Kukai enshrined the goddess Niutsu, her son Kariba, and more than 100 *kami* deities from around Mt. Koya as the protector deities of that mountain. Legend has it that the *myojin* [kami] Kariba, the spirit of Mt. Koya, offered his two companion dogs, "Shiro" ("White") and "Kuro" ("Black") to assist Kukai in finding the preordained site where he was to construct his monastery. In order to venerate these *kami*, Kukai built a special shrine, *Miyashiro*, in the heart of the monastic compound at Mt. Koya.

Another approach to reconciling Shinto and Buddhism was the theory of "essence-manifestation," or *honji-suijaku*, which became popular in the tenth century in Japan. According to this theory, the *kami* were considered manifestations of the Buddha essence. For example, the *kami* of the sacred mountain Kumano came to be called "Gongen," meaning the "provisional manifestation of the Buddha essence in the guise of *kami*.". . . Gradually, one-to-one correspondence between a *kami* and a particular Buddha or Bodhisattva was drawn up. The sun goddess Amaterasu was identified as the manifestation of the sun Buddha, Mahavairochana; the god Hachiman was the manifestation of Amida Buddha; the goddess of the Itsukushima Shrine (which was the tutelage shrine of the Taira, or Heike, clan) was the manifestation of Kannon, and so forth. Every *kami* now had a corresponding Buddhist "origin." Under the influence of Buddhism, images of *kami* fashioned after those of Buddhas and Bodhisattvas, were created and venerated at Shinto shrines.

The most salient case of the hybrid nature of Buddhism and Shinto was Ryobu Shinto. With ryobu meaning "twofold," "double," or "dual," the idea was derived from the Shingon view of the worlds in terms of the womb mandala and the diamond mandala [two related Buddhist sacred symbols intended to aid the search for enlightenment]. Ryobu Shinto identified Mahavairochana of the Shingon doctrine with Izanagi and Izanami [Shinto's founding deities] . . . ; it also considered the Inner Shrine of Ise as corresponding to the womb mandala, and the Outer Shrine to the diamond mandala.

The spiritual fervor of the Kamakura period [1192–1333] . . . entailed not only the founding of new Buddhist sects but also an awakening of Shinto. Its adher-

The giant bronze Buddha in Kamakura, near Tokyo, was cast in 1252 during an era of spiritual fervor.

ents now advocated the "reverse theory of essence-manifestation." Placing the Shinto deities above the Buddhas and Bodhisattvas, they claimed that the *kami* deities were the original essence and that Buddhas and Bodhisattvas were the provisional manifestations of the *kami* essence. This shift in the balance of power between Buddhism and Shinto signaled the beginning of a move to articulate and systematize Shinto doctrines.

The Emperor and Empress as Living *Kami*

The status of Shinto shrines was elevated in the mid-seventh century, under the patronage of Emperor

Tenmu (r. 673–86) and Empress Jito (r. 686–97). It was Emperor Tenmu who ordered the compilation of the early Japanese history, which resulted in the *Kojiki* (712) and the *Nihongi* (720). He also offered imperial protection to major shrines, and in 674 he personally paid a visit to the Ise Shrine as his ancestor shrine. A religio-ideological move to identify the imperial family as the descendants of Amaterasu was then underway. The link between the reigning emperor or empress and Amaterasu was readily drawn, since ancient kings and queens had often been endowed with shamanic power and functioned as high priests and priestesses. Both Emperor Tenmu and Empress Jito were described by the court poets as living *kami*. This association between the imperial family and Shinto mythology would become the core ideology of Japanese nationalism; and as such it constitutes a sensitive issue for many Japanese today. . . .

The confidence of the Shintoists was boosted by the Japanese victory over Mongol invading forces [Central Asian warriors who had already conquered China and Korea] in 1274 and 1281. On both occasions, opportune typhoons swiftly and decisively sank the invaders' ships and killed many of their troops. The belief spread that Japan was protected by the *kami* deities, who would send a divine wind (*shinpu* or *kamikaze*) at times of national crisis. From then on, whenever Japan came under threat by foreign powers, the typical response of the Japanese ruler would be to declare that "Japan is the country of *kami*."

This idea that Japan was a divinely protected country grew during the Muromachi period [1336–1573], based on the account of the unbroken line of the imperial succession since the "Age of the Gods." This view was brought to the fore by the learned warrior Kitabatake Chikafusa (1293–1354), a staunch supporter of the southern imperial court, during the period when Japan had two emperors, each claiming legitimacy (1334–92). In his *Records of the Legitimate Succession of the Divine Sovereigns* (*Jin'no shotoki*, 1339), Kitabatake declared: "Japan is the divine country [*shinkoku*]. The heavenly ancestor [i.e., the deity Kunitokotachi] it was who first laid its foundations, and the Sun Goddess left her descendants to reign over it forever and ever. This is true only of our country, and nothing similar may be found in foreign lands." He borrowed from Confucianism to describe the moral virtues of the three regalia, the symbol of imperial authority: the mirror stood for honesty, the jewel for compassion (since it can sway and covers a wide area), and the sword for courage (as needed in making decisions). Kitabatake's attempt to give a systematic explanation to Shinto symbolism encouraged the further development of Shinto theology.

Kitabatake's claim had a textual basis in the works of Watarai Yukitada (1236–1305), a Shinto priest of the Outer Shrine of Ise. He described various facets of Shinto tradition, such as the history of *sengu* [the rebuilding of shrines every twenty years] . . ., and of Shinto symbolism, including the meaning of the evergreen *sakaki* (a sacred tree in Shinto because it is an example of something that fully receives the cosmic energy, or blessings of the *kami*, regardless of the season).

Yoshida Kanetomo (1435–1511), head priest of the Yoshida Shrine in Kyoto, further developed Watarai's line of work. He asserted the primacy of Shinto over Buddhism by way of the "reverse essence-manifestation" theory. Yoshida took the example of a tree as a metaphor and explained that Shinto was the root and the trunk of all truth, Confucianism the branches and leaves, and Buddhism the fruit of the tree. He asserted that, in addition to the kinds of Shinto that had been amalgamated with Buddhism or woven into the esoteric Buddhist worldview, there was a pure, unadulterated core Shinto, a "primal Shinto," which was devoid of the influence of Confucianism, Buddhism, and Daoism. Works by Watarai and Yoshida were early attempts to free Shinto from the yoke of Buddhism, and to assert its independence.

Development of Popular Piety

The assertion that Shinto was an independent religion gave local Shinto shrines the impetus to gain more followers during the Muromachi period. The strategy of the Shinto clergy was to promote the message of longevity, health, military victory (to warriors), profits (to merchants), rich harvests (to peasants), and bounties (to fishermen)—all in exchange for their worshipping their *kami*. The accent was on "profit here and now" (*gense riyaku*). This idea appealed to people, and the popular belief in deities of good luck (*fukujin*) spread. Especially popular were the gods Ebisu (the god of fishing and commerce), Daikoku (the god of wealth, a kind of Japanese "Santa Claus"), and Bishamon (the god of wealth and power). Many of these deities are still revered today among those who make their living by fishing, farming, and commerce. In the spirit of "profit here and now," pilgrimage to the Ise Shrine also became extremely meritorious.

Japan's Samurai Warriors Lived in an Era of Religious Integration

by Louis Frederic

The Heian period of Japanese history (794–1185) was followed by over four centuries characterized by frequent conflict among warring noble families. And while earlier the dominant person in Japan was the emperor, in this new era it was a figure known as the shogun, a word that might be translated as the "emperor's military adviser." The nation continued to have emperors, who continued to be enshrined according to Shinto rituals, but it was the shoguns who truly ruled while the emperors were relegated to the background. Shoguns themselves, meanwhile, generally came from whichever warring family was able to establish temporary dominance. Often helping shoguns and their competitors were bands of samurai, the warriors of medieval Japan. Trained under and living according to a strict code known as Bushido (the way of the warrior), the samurai were not only highly skilled fighters, they were expected to be religiously devout as well.

In the following selection author Louis Frederic examines the religious context in which samurai warriors lived. It was influenced by many sects of Buddhism, such as the popular Pure Land sect, which revered an enlightened figure, or Buddha, known as Amida, and Zen, which emphasized meditation. But the samurai also observed Shinto rituals and studied Confucianism, the Chinese philosophy of social and earthly harmony characterized by, among other things, yin-yang, or the balance of opposites. In such ways the samurai reflected the religious diversity and syncretism of medieval Japan. Louis Frederic is the author of the *Encyclopedia of Asian Civilizations* and the *Japan Encyclopedia*.

The appearance on the Japanese scene of a new system of government, in complete contrast to that practised until then by the aristocrats of Kyôto, offered, from the spiritual and moral point of view, a kind of liberation which enabled new ideas to gain ground, and religions and philosophies to develop and win over the people. Many new ways of thought were superimposed on to traditional Japanese Buddhism, a form of Buddhism that was a blend of Shintô practices and beliefs of Chinese origin—the development of the pietist theories of Amidism [Pure Land Buddhism], the uncompromising theories of [Buddhist reformer] Nichiren and the meditative theories of Zen [Buddhism]. The samurai class adopted a Confucian moral philosophy, and the revival of Shintô cults was purely Japanese. Powerful personalities provided a stimulus for the religious spirit of the Japanese people. Tempered by religion and spiritualized by Zen philosophy, the samurai spirit breathed strength into the new sects.

It cannot be said that there is a Japanese Buddhism, but rather that there are several kinds of Buddhism in Japan. If the nobles of Kyôto practised a form of Buddhism in which rites played a very important part, the samurai retained primarily philosophical concepts such as the one that emphasized the impermanence of all things. The masses saw in Buddhism only divinities to be worshipped, for the same reason as the *kami*, the spirits of the fields and mountains. As for the priests, their conceptions of Buddhism differed according to the sect to which they belonged.

The Japanese, traditionally tolerant from the religious point of view and as accommodating with regard to divinities as to foreign beliefs, never formulated any positive dogma, nor enforced recognition of any exclusive cult. They did their utmost to extract from each belief or philosophy, on the one hand ideas which seemed to them essential and valid to all, and on the other those which, fitting in with their own way of life, were likely to satisfy them morally and spiritually. This was only possible if, to the Japanese way of thinking, the sacred was regarded as something entirely different from the profane—which was indeed the case, although at certain times and in certain circumstances it might be difficult to separate the two. But here the Japanese reacted in their own way, by avoiding mixing elements which at first sight, appeared to them incompatible, and by juxtaposing them. In this way the majority of Japanese could at the same time be Shintôists, Buddhists and Confucians. At the end of the sixteenth century, they were all these, and sometimes Christians into the bargain.

Keeping Both Shintô and Buddhist Beliefs

The samurai, whose warrior code compelled him to kill, to eat meat, in a word (and according to religious ethics) to injure his neighbour, might seem to be in complete contradiction to the Buddhist teachings which forbade the taking of life. Nevertheless, he worshipped in the first place the ancestral gods of his clan or his family and the *kami* who protected both himself and his fellow men; in this respect he was Shintôist. The samurai also observed the moral principles of obedience, loyalty and filial piety which were derived from the Confucian system of ethics. He worshipped the Buddhist divinities, he believed in universal impermanence, in retribution of good and evil in a future life, and in a paradisian life after death and, in this, he could claim to be Buddhist. Yoritomo [a shogun of the period 1185–1189], while worshipping Hachiman [the *kami* of battle], his *ujigami* (clan god), was at the same time a fervent Buddhist. There is even a tradition that he never set out to do battle without fixing a small image of Kannon [the Buddhist goddess of mercy] in his hair-knot beforehand and that he was never without his rosary for saying Buddhist prayers. And no matter how faithful a devotee of the *kami* of his clan, how mighty a slayer of enemies and cutter-off of heads a samurai was, he might all of a sudden retire to a monastery and become a monk.

For what mattered most of all to the Japanese was to have, after a very full life, what they called a 'good death' (*ojô*) guaranteeing their rebirth in the [Buddhist] Paradise of Amida. On the other hand, monks who considered themselves losers as far as their material interests were concerned, did not hesitate to go to war and to behave like coarse ruffians, at the same time reciting *sûtra* [Buddhist scriptures]. An imperial prince, Morinaga, chief abbot of the Tendai monastery on Mount Hiei, when pursued by his enemies, recited incantations to a god in order to render himself invisible:

> In the hall of the Buddha, he saw three large Chinese chests on legs, containing scrolls of the *Daihannya* (sûtra) and left open at the place where a monk had started reading them. The lids of two of the chests

A samurai warrior fends off arrows in this nineteenth-century woodblock print.

were still closed. However, more than half the Sacred
Scripture scrolls had been taken out of the one that
was left open. The prince slipped inside this open
box, pulled the Sacred Scrolls down over him and
silently recited incantations so that he might be hid-
den from the sight of men. He held the cold steel of
a dagger against his abdomen thinking: 'If they find
me, I shall take my life.'

This miscellany of beliefs, these seeming contradic-
tions, likely to amaze a Westerner used to more dog-
matic coherence, are natural to a people for whom the
idea of heresy does not exist. The religious outlook of
the Japanese was essentially fluid, making it possible for
them to identify the *kami* of the soil with the imported
divinities of Buddhism. Their way of thinking did not
necessarily at this time affect their way of life. . . .

Changes from Early Shintô

Shintô, the Way of the Kami, the earliest form of religion in Japan, had undergone many changes since the
ninth century, a time when her divinities had been put
on the same footing as those of Buddhism, Buddha the
Great Illuminator, or Dainichi Nyorai . . . being declared identical with Amaterasu Omikami, Kami of the
Sun and ancestor of the line of Tennô, or emperors. The
Japanese were at times unable to make clear distinctions between Buddhism and Shintô, unless it was in
the division of labour; upon Buddhism devolved everything concerning life after death, while Shintô turned
its attention more particularly to life here on earth. All
events relating to this life, birth, marriage, battles, festivals, were regarded as falling within the province of
Shintô, or rather of the kami, whom it was advisable to
inform and propitiate on every occasion, either by pu-

rifications (*harai*) or by offerings, dances and ritual invocations (*norito*).

But the increasingly sumptuous ceremonies of the Buddhist cult had made Shintô appear to be a religion of somewhat minor importance and, during the periods of ruthless conflicts between the Buddhist sects, the cult of the kami, although still observed in country districts and among the warrior class, seemed to have lost its autonomy. This was primarily due to the fact that there was no clearly defined concept of kami, the Japanese being 'intuitively aware of the kami in their inmost beings and communicating with them directly without ever having formed any clear notion of the kami, conceptually as theologically' [according to Japanese religious scholar Dr. Ono Sokyo]. And if Shintô has a mythology or even several which describe the activities of a multitude of kami, there is no absolute deity among them. Each kami has its own nature, considered as the 'spirit' of an object or a place, of an element or a phenomenon, a spirit which is 'the' object or 'the' phenomenon, or considered as protector of a group, of a clan (*ujigami*), or even of a family or again of a specific place. As such the kami are reputed to protect individuals as well as the whole country. When the typhoon of 1281 had destroyed the Mongol fleet, Fujiwara-no-Tameuji, the imperial messenger sent to the temple of Ise to thank the goddess Amaterasu, composed a *waka* [thirty-one-syllable poem, also called *tanka*] in her honour:

> In answer to our fervent prayers for the
>   favour of the Heavens,
> Our goddess, stirred by divine wrath
> Has swept the seas of the mighty enemy fleet
> And his ships are destroyed and shattered.

Shintô, having neither Sacred Scriptures nor dogma,

cannot claim to replace Buddhism, which provided the people with a moral and a religious philosophy. For in Shintô there is no precise distinction between Good and Evil. This distinction depends upon circumstances. Man's soul is innately good and he only commits evil when he is momentarily out of harmony with Nature, with the Kami, because he is 'unclean'. And evil is sometimes regarded as a sickness which affects a human being temporarily, a sickness mainly due to a state of uncleanness which cuts him off from the world of the kami and which it is essential to eliminate by purifications. Nevertheless, despite the increasing ascendancy of Buddhism, Shintô remained inextricably bound up with the customs as with the ways of thinking and of living of the Japanese people. So it was that promises made among samurai and written under oath, brought various Shintô divinities into play depending upon clans, Hachiman in the case of the Genji, Hakone Gongen, and Izusan Gongen; Mishima Daimyôjin in the case of the Hôjô (of Taira stock); and that [shogun] Hideyoshi in 1591 could write to the viceroy of Goa, though the intermediary of a Jesuit missionary:

> Our country is the country of the kami, and kami is the spirit. Everything in Nature comes into being through the spirit. There can be no spirituality without the kami. There is no Way without the kami. Kami reigns in times of prosperity as in times of adversity. Kami is positive and negative and unfathomable. Thus kami is the source of all existence. Buddhism in India, Confucianism in China and Shintô in Japan all proclaim it. To understand Shintô is to understand Buddhism as well as Confucianism. . . .

Shintô, in close relationship with most of the festivals observed by the Japanese people, with farming activities as with important events affecting everyday life, played its part in no small way in the formation of Japanese Buddhism from the time this was adopted by the common people; and it gave to it a particular character. In the same way it is very probable that Zen [Buddhism] itself would not have been likely to take root in Japan if minds had not been trained for a long time by Shintô to an intuitive understanding of Nature and its mysteries, and if they had not been used to communicating with the divine without having recourse to dogmas or complicated rites. In this sense, it is even possible to state that conceptions of an aesthetic nature attributed solely to Zen, are in actual fact typically Japanese, and that they were only revealed by Zen. Indeed, Zen in Japan seems to us to be like a spiritualized form of Shintô more than a purely Buddhist sect.

Adding Confucianism to the Mix

With Buddhism (and perhaps even before it) a number of Chinese beliefs made their appearance in Japan, beliefs belonging to the philosophical systems of Confucius and Lao-Tzu [founder of Taoism]. The study of the Chinese classics helped to spread Confucian and Taoïst concepts among the more lettered Japanese, concepts which had a profound enough influence on their lives to change them appreciably. The bakufu [learned] samurai themselves took examples of heroism from these classics (such as the *Analects* [of Confucius]) and from treatises on military history which laid down as a basic principle that 'World peace cannot be ensured except by force and might of arms.' Yoshitsune [general and younger brother of Yoritomo] tried by every means in his power to obtain a secret treatise on military science entitled *Liu-t'ao*, in the possession of a learned nobleman, in order to learn the Chinese art of warfare. Commentators of the Song epoch [in China, 960–1279], in particular Chu-Hsi (1130–1200), imparted a new vitality to Chinese Confucianism and, thanks to Chinese monks who came to Japan, the doctrines of Chu-Hsi's neo-Confucianism, which flourished throughout the Middle Ages, were to continue to do so still under the rule of the Tokugawa [clan, 1600–1868]. Learning, 'Knowledge needing to implement Faith', was the first essential of right conduct. The Zen monks, almost in spite of themselves, were active propagators of Confucian ideas; these were adopted by the rich and idle classes as well as by the influential warriors of the Ashikagas' [shoguns who ruled from 1336–1573] entourage. Many other Chinese beliefs (among them those connected with Taoism) had supporters in Japan, and the Zen monks saw in Lao-Tzu's outlook 'To act by doing nothing' a kind of parallel to their own 'absence of system'. These various Chinese beliefs had also influenced Shintô and introduced into Japan, long ago, theories on dualism and divinatory practices in vogue at the Court. These were codified by the '*Yang* and *Yin* Bureau', the *Ommyôr-yô*, which also controlled astrological observances. At first confined to the aristocratic circles of Kyôto, these had finally influenced the commoners who conformed to customs whose meaning they did not understand because 'for the greater number, the feeling that was bound up with *Ommyô-dô* divinities (*yang* and *yin*) was mainly based on the fear of misfortune and the search after good fortune.'

Although for greater clarity we have been obliged to deal with each sect or religion separately here, it must not be forgotten that in Japan, especially during the Middle Ages, syncretism was the rule everywhere, even in the case of the uncompromising [Buddhist reformer] Nichiren: no doctrine is altogether pure, no believer belongs exclusively to a single faith or a single doctrine. The most ardent Amadist [Amida Buddhist] will also be a believer in Shintô, the Zen monk will at the same time be a follower of Confucian concepts, and the common man will follow all the cults to a certain extent, although he claims to be an adherent of this one or that one. And even the most intolerant of Nichirenites will not fail to worship the kami. For the Japanese cannot conceive of one thing being good to the exclusion of all others. With deliberate irony, he will find that every dogma has its good qualities and its faults:

> Zen likes sweeping,
> Shingon cooks,
> Monto (Jôdo-Shinshü) delights in flowers
> As Hokke in offerings
> While Jôdo has neither rhyme nor reason,

declares an old proverb in *tanka* [thirty-one-syllable] form, in caricature of the main sects.

Under Buddhist Influence, Shinto Thinking Became More Sophisticated

by Robert N. Bellah

As Japanese elites adopted Buddhism in increasing numbers in the Nara and Heian periods of Japanese history (710–1185), and as Buddhism continued to flourish in Japan's middle ages (1185–1603), Shinto remained mostly a folk religion, practiced by ordinary, uneducated people. But in the thirteenth century, and perhaps earlier, Shinto priests and scholars began to add more sophisticated philosophical elements to folk Shinto. They were influenced in this by Buddhist thinking, as Robert N. Bellah, the author of the following selection, suggests. But they also helped to transform Shinto into a faith comparable on a philosophical level with Buddhism. One way in which Shintoists accomplished this was to emphasize inner purity of the mind, as opposed to the outer purity reflected in such Shinto customs as washing before worship or avoiding menstruating women. The process of refining Shinto thought continued into the Tokugawa era of 1600–1868. Robert N. Bellah is professor emeritus of sociology at the University of California–Berkeley.

Fertility, purification, and similar forms of ritual continued down to recent times in more or less the same "primitive" forms . . . but beginning at least as early as the 13th century there developed, especially around [Shintō's] cult center at Ise, a marked trend to philosophical and ethical rationalization. There is no doubt that this occurred under the stimulus of Buddhist influence, but it is a genuine reworking of the Shintō tradition and not merely a Buddhist overlay.

One of the earliest documents which reveals this trend is the *Shintō Gobusho* compiled by the Gekū [outer shrine] priests of Ise probably in the 13th century, some of its materials undoubtedly being of even earlier date. With respect to offerings it says, "The gods desire not material gifts, but offerings of uprightness and sincerity," and with respect to purity, "To do good is to be pure; to commit evil is to be impure. The deities dislike evil deeds, because they are impure." The [Buddhist] monk Musō-Kokushi (1271–1340) recounts a visit to the Ise shrine not long after the period of the presumed compilation of the *Shintō Gobusho*. His account is as follows:

> At the Ise Daijingū offerings are not allowed, neither is the reading of any Buddhist sutra or incantation. When I went to Ise I stopped for a while near the Gekū and questioned a Shintō ritualist styled Negi whom I met there on this point and he said, "When anyone comes here to worship there is both an outer and an inner purity. The former consists in eating clean food and observing the ritual purification and keeping oneself from defilement, but the latter means ridding the mind of all ambitious desire." The usual thing is to make offerings at shrines and have *Kagura* performances held in order to petition the deities for some benefits that are desired, which is very far from inward purity and so is declined here.

Here we can see how the old ideas of offerings and purification are given ethical and symbolic significance. The implication of this idea of inner purity for the relation of man to the divine is brought out in the following quote from a 14th century visitor to the Ise shrine:

> And particularly is it the deep-rooted custom of this shrine that we should bring no Buddhist rosary or offering or any special petition in our hearts and this is called "Inner Purity." Washing in sea water and keeping the body free from all defilements is called "Outer Purity." And when both these purities are attained there is then no barrier between our mind and that of the deity. And if we feel to become thus one with the divine, what more do we need to pray for? When I heard that this was the true way of worshipping at the shrine, I could not refrain from shedding tears of gratitude.

The earlier notion of deity [as a sort of guardian spirit], one that continues to be held down to modern times, is in the above passage tending to be replaced by the second concept of the divine [in which the divine is characterized as an abstract force, or as the "essential reality."] . . . This is clearly brought out in a statement by the 14th century Shintō theologian Imbe-no-Masamichi in his *Shindai Kuketsu* (1367):

> *Kami* [the native Japanese word for deity] is from *kagami* [mirror]. This is abbreviated and read *Kami*. The Divine Mind, like a clear mirror, reflects all things in nature. It operates with impartial justice and tolerates not a single spot of uncleanness. That which in Heaven is *Kami*, in nature is Spirit and in man is Sincerity. If the spirit of nature and the heart of man are pure and clear, then they are *Kami*.

To round out the discussion we may turn to a very popular Shintō work of the Tokugawa Period, the *Warongo* or *Japanese Analects*. In the following quote we can detect both of the basic conceptions of deity and the final assertion of the pre-eminence of inner over outer purity:

> That the God dislikes what is unclean, is equivalent to saying that a person who is impure in heart displeases God.
>
> He that is honest and upright in heart is not unclean, even though he be not ceremoniously so in body.
>
> To God, inward purity is all important; mere external cleanliness avails not. This is because God is the Essential Uprightness and Honesty, and therefore, it is His Heavenly Ordinance that we should lead an honest and happy life in harmony with the Divine Will.
>
> If a man is pure in heart, rest assured that he will ever feel the Divine Presence with him, and possess the immediate sense of the Divine within him.

A German Traveler Describes a Seventeenth-Century Pilgrimage to Ise, Shinto's Great Shrine

by Engelbert Kaempfer

The first Europeans to reach Japan were Portuguese traders, who arrived in the mid-1500s. They were followed by other merchants and Roman Catholic missionaries from numerous European countries. The traders had initial success, and the missionaries found that their faith appealed to many people in this land associated with Shinto and Buddhism; by 1579 there were an estimated 130,000 Christians in Japan.

When the Tokugawa clan firmly established itself as the leading family of the country in 1600, however, Japan's attitude toward European visitors and their religion changed. The new leaders saw Europeans as a potential threat to the stability of their new regime, established after more than a century of bloodshed known in Japanese history as the "century of the people at war." By 1640 all European missionaries and merchants had been expelled from Japan and Japanese Christians were forced to give up their new faith. The only Europeans who were allowed to come to the country were those who came on one of the two Dutch ships the

Engelbert Kaempfer, *Kaempfer's Japan: Tokugawa Culture Observed*, ed. and trans. Beatrice M. Bodart-Bailey. Honolulu: University of Hawaii Press, 1999.

Japanese allowed to land each year at the port of Nagasaki. These restrictions remained in place until 1853.

Representatives of the Dutch visitors were expected to make an annual pilgrimage to Edo (later called Tokyo), the capital of Tokugawa Japan, to pay their respects to the shogun. In 1691 and 1692 a German doctor and scholar named Engelbert Kaempfer accompanied the Dutch on their travels across Japan, keeping a detailed diary. The following selection comes from his account of his travels, first published in 1727. It is his description of how both high- and lowborn Japanese conducted their pilgrimage to Ise (pronounced "ee-say"), the greatest of all Shinto shrines. Located near the ancient capital of Nara, Ise's "outer" shrine is devoted to Toyouke, the goddess of the harvest, while it's "inner" shrine is devoted to the sun goddess, Amaterasu.

A variety of pilgrimages are conducted by this nation. The first, and most important, is to Ise; the second, a visit to the thirty-three most important Kannon [Buddhist goddess of mercy] temples of this empire; the third is made to some of the most important *shin* (*kami*) [Shinto] or *hotoke* (*butsu*) [Buddhist] temples throughout the country which have performed miracles and given help to their worshippers. The most famous of these are: Nikkō *dera*, which means "sunlight temple," in the province of Ōshū, Hachiman, and so forth, the temples of the teacher Yakushi, or other ancient and important temples esteemed as places of worship and penance, according to people's own preference. A true Shinto believer goes only to Shinto temples, such as Dazaifu in Chikuzen, where Tenjin [an

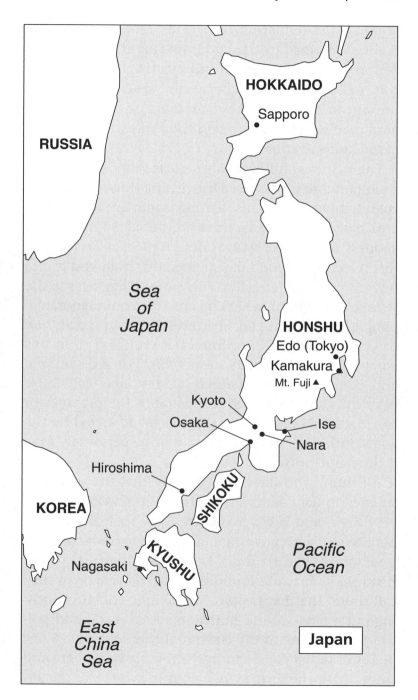

RUSSIA

HOKKAIDO

Sapporo

Sea
of
Japan

HONSHU

Edo (Tokyo)

Kamakura

Mt. Fuji ▲

Kyoto

Osaka

Ise

Nara

Hiroshima

SHIKOKU

KOREA

KYUSHU

Nagasaki

Pacific
Ocean

East
China
Sea

Japan

important statesman] died. The last kind of pilgrimage is also performed by the Buddhists; in other words, it is performed by believers from both religions, but each goes to his own gods. The second kind of pilgrimage belongs to neither of the main religions, but the common man believes this to be a good way to obtain prosperity and salvation.

The first is as follows: *sangū* means literally "visiting a temple" and is only used for visiting this, the most sacred temple [Ise]. This temple commemorates their greatest god, Tenshō daijin, or Tenshō kōdaijin [the sun goddess Amaterasu, who is described in male form in this selection], which means literally "high god of the heavenly clan of terrestrial emperors." They refer to the temple as Daijingū, which means "the commemorative temple of the great god," because *dai* means great; *shin* or *kami*, a spirit, god, or immortal soul; and *gū* in this combination and others means *miya*, or a devotional and commemorative temple. Commoners call it Ise *miya* in accordance with the name of the province of Ise. They believe that the site was made sacred by the god's birth, life, and death and that he personally gave it the name of Ise.

All those who have visited it say that the temple is situated in flat country, is poorly built of wood and not very high, and is covered with a low roof of hay. It is maintained with great care in the image of the original poor temple of early times, built in their poverty by the first inhabitants and founders of this nation, or, as they call them, the first people. The temple contains nothing but a large, round mirror, made of metal and polished (according to the custom of this country). A few pieces of white paper cut into strips are hung here and there. With the former they wish to symbolize the all-encompassing knowledge and glory of the god, with the latter, the cleanliness of the site. At the same time, it cautions worshippers not to step in front of the god unless their hearts and bodies are clean.

Shrine Priests and Guardians

The temple has various chapels in honor of lesser gods, numbering nearly one hundred, which, however, are only shaped like a temple and are often so small that nobody could possibly enter. Each has only one *kannushi* [guardian priest] to guard it. Close by live the many *negi*, or lords of temples, or, as they call themselves, *tayū*, meaning "ambassador" or "evangelist," who maintain large houses and lodges to accommodate the travelers. Not far away is the city or town, also carrying the name of the sacred site of Ise. It has many inns, print shops, paper makers, book binders, and builders of shrines, all necessary for this holy industry.

Every honest *shinja* [literally, Shintoist], or rather, every patriot whatever his belief, should visit this sacred site annually, or, at the very least, once in his life, to show due gratitude to the god and founder of his nation by this act of homage. Also, cleansed by this act of all sins, he may enter a happy state after death, or, in the naive eyes of the uneducated masses, he may be blessed with bodily health, food and drink, money, clothing, children, and a family. To strengthen this belief, every visitor personally receives from the *tayū* a box with a letter of indulgence, called *ōharai*, which means "great purification." People who are unable to obtain this personally because of their occupation, illness, or age can buy one annually. In addition to the above *shinshū* [Shintoists], one also sees other Buddhists because they wish to claim the right to be called honest patriots and there-fore visit this place of their founder once or several times in their lives. There are also many Buddhists who stay at home but annually purchase the *ōharai* from Ise and, in addition, an annual letter of indulgence from their priest.

This journey is undertaken throughout the year, but especially during the first three months because of the good weather, and is made by young and old, rich and poor, men and women, but people of high rank seldom make it personally.

The shogun pays his respects to this site by means of an ordinary, annual embassy leaving in the first month, while at the same time another is sent to the *dairi* [impe-rial court]. Other barons and territorial lords do likewise. Rich people make do on their own money; others man-age by begging and walking on foot. They carry a rolled-up straw mat on their back as a cover at night, have a walking stick in their hand, and a water ladle tucked into their belt, with which they also collect alms, baring their heads in European fashion. They wear a wide-brimmed traveling hat made of plaited split reed, which, like the water ladle, is marked with their name as well as that of their birthplace or residence, so that they can be identified if they suddenly die on the road. Others of some wealth wear a short white robe without sleeves over their clothes, on which the above names are printed on the chest and back. One meets several hun-dred of such pilgrims daily. They come in great numbers from the province of Ōshū and the shogunal city of Edo, where often the children run away from their parents to make this pilgrimage. If other parts of the country were visited without a pass, people would run into consider-able trouble to the point of risking their lives, but everyday custom provides the liberty that the *ōharai* serves as a pass and is considered enough.

After a pilgrim has left home, his family puts a straw rope over the front door, from which hang twisted strips of cut paper to indicate purity, so that nobody with a heavy *imi* will enter (that is, people who are impure because of the death of their parents). For it has been noticed that at that time pilgrims encounter misfortune or problems; also they may have bad and disturbing dreams. Such symbols of purity are also put up across an avenue that leads to a *miya*.

On this pilgrimage people must practice greater abstinence than ordinarily. Both going and coming back they must refrain from sexual intercourse, which otherwise neither the gods nor the people of this nation seem to consider in any way unholy. Consequently the only punishment it brings is that the parties remain stuck to each other until a potent ceremony by one of their *yamabushi*, one kind of hermit, or another powerful Buddhist priest, permits them to come apart. People strongly believe in this, for they claim that cases happen every year. People who are *fujō*, or unclean, may not show themselves here. If they dare to do so, they and their family would be visited with *shinbatsu*, or revenge of the gods. A *shukke* is a priest of the Buddhist religion, and since he is practicing an impure profession by taking care of the dying and funerals, he may never ever appear here.

Paying Respects

After a pilgrim has reached this location—which is visited daily by great numbers, amounting, on some days, to several thousands—he goes to the home of one or

the other *kannushi* from whom he annually receives his
indulgence as his acquaintance and delivers his greet-
ings, courteously bending down to the floor. On the
same or the following day, the *kannushi* in person either
leads him and others who have announced their arrival
at his house around the sacred site or asks a servant to
do so. He briefly mentions the names of the temples
and gods, and finally takes him in front of the middle
and main temple of Tenshō daijin, where he has him
pay his humble respects, kneeling with his forehead
touching the ground, and people pray for good health
or anything else according to their concerns. After this
procession has been completed, the pilgrim is enter-
tained by the *kannushi* either on the same day or, if his
devotions have taken longer, on the following days.
Also, if pilgrims cannot afford the public inns, he will
put them up for the night. But however poor they are,
they will make a generous donation from the alms they
themselves received, which is never refused.

After the pilgrims' worship has been completed, this
kannushi hands everybody an indulgence. It is a poor,
small, square box, the length of a fan or one and a half
spans, two inches wide, and the depth of one and a half
thumbs, made of thin boards tacked together. Inside it
has a bundle of thin, small sticks of the same material
and length, some with clean paper strips tied around:
all of it is miserable merchandise purchased for a miserable sum to commend to people that humbleness
and cleanliness are virtues esteemed by their gods. A
printed piece of paper is pasted on the front of the box.
The name of this temple, Daijingū, meaning temple of
the great god, is printed in beautiful characters, and at
the end in small characters is the name of the *kannushi*
who has issued this *ōharai* (for there are many who take

people around), with the added title of *tayū*, which means ambassador, or evangelist, an honorific title commonly used by those serving at a *miya*.

As soon as a pilgrim on foot has received this *ōharai*, with the greatest deference, he attaches the same under his traveling hat over his forehead to protect it from rain. For convenience sake, a bundle of straw of the same weight is attached to the other side. People traveling on horseback have room to keep it in a better place. When pilgrims return home with such an *ōharai*, it is kept as a sacred object throughout the year. After that period is over, it is relegated to another honest place as if its potency had evaporated like smoke. Every year it is put on a board above the height of a man, attached to the wall of a clean room for this purpose. In some cities they are attached to the front of the house, above the door under the front roof. People living in poor accommodations have no cleaner place than a tree in their backyard. This is also where it is placed if one finds a lost *ōharai*, or that of a dead person, on the road.

In order to render service to those who desire this sacred object, and wish to, but cannot, travel as described above, the *kannushi* from Ise annually send large packs and boxes of this merchandise to the cities and villages of all provinces. It is taken by certain emissaries who arrange their journey so that they reach the most important places at *shōgatsu*, the New Year's celebrations, a festival of the most solemn rites of purification. At the same time they bring new calendars, which can be made only by the *mikado* [emperor] and can be printed only at the above location. The envoy gets one mace or one *bu* [coin] for both pieces and sometimes, but rarely, more, according to each person's wealth and preference. People who accept this merchandise once are annually burdened with it, and the next year will again receive three items: one receipt in the shape of a note of appreciation addressed to the purchaser, a new *ōharai*, and thirdly also a new calendar. If he has given a generous donation, which, however, is rarely done by ordinary citizens, he will also be rewarded with a *sakazuki*, a wooden, lacquered drinking bowl.

Ichinohe [the supposed author of a travel guide] describes the situation of the Ise *miya* as follows: There are two Ise temples situated about twelve streets distant, one behind the other. Both are poor, the size of about six mats, with *kannushi* sitting inside as guardians and out of respect for Tenshō daijin. Both temples are covered with hay and are poor but have been built without the slightest scratch to the skin. They are of equal importance, but the proper and real chapel of the deity is further at the back on higher ground. This chapel is called *hongū*, which means "real temple" (just as Suwa in Nagasaki is also on higher ground). Both are hung with some mirrors and papers inside.

The first *miya*, called *gekū* [outer shrine], has many *kannushi* and eighty *massha*, which are small temples of lesser importance for the lesser deities placed around, each the size of four mats, with a *kannushi* as guardian and collector of alms, which he keeps for himself.

The second *miya*, which is some twelve streets further away, is called *naigū* [inner shrine] and has forty *massha* with their *kannushi* guardians. All guardians of *massha* are called *miya suzume*, which means "temple sparrows."

Meticulous people who want to inspect the temples do this first without the guidance of a *kannushi* and proceed as follows. From the city of Ise they first go to the river Miyagawa, which flows past the city on the side facing Ise *miya*, and bravely wash in it. Having cleansed themselves, they pass through and go beyond the living quarters of the *kannushi* and other merchants situated some three or four streets away from the river and, continuing over sandy terrain, head straight for the *gekū miya*. Having paid their respects, they continue along the right to inspect the *massha* and then return to the previous location. Then they proceed to the other temple of Tenshō daijin called *naigū*. After paying their respects, they do the same tour to pay respect to the surrounding *massha*. Then they head for the hills for some fifteen streets to a mountain situated above and near the raised ocean shore, to pay respect to a little cave called *ama no iwato* (situated some twenty *ken* [about forty yards] from the sea), which means "heavenly shore." Here Tenshō daijin hid himself and by secluding himself deprived the world and other planets of light, proving beyond doubt that he was the lord of light and the most important of the gods. The cave is some one-and-a-half mats large. It has a chapel with a *kami* sitting on a cow called Dainichi nyorai, which means great embodiment of the sun, as object of worship. Also here some *kannushi*, who live in two houses above the raised seashore, are waiting. To commemorate his visit, the caller has a little *sugi* sapling planted there (for a few coins). From these tall shores, you can see, at a distance of one and a half miles, a large island that is supposed to have been created in the age of Tenshō daijin.

After this tour of inspection, enthusiasts turn right, proceeding inland for two miles, and inspect a beautiful *butsu dō* temple [Buddhist] called Asamadake, where they pay their respects to a Kannon [or bodhisattva] called Kokuzō bosatsu, and then return to the town of Ise.

A Shinto Teacher Prescribes Laughter as a Source of Purification

by Munetada Kurozumi

In the early decades of the 1800s Shinto was revived in Japan, a reaction to both the Buddhist preoccupations of many Tokugawa leaders and the uncertainty caused by increased urbanization and economic centralization. Shinto, which had never disappeared and continued to be a part of daily life for most ordinary Japanese, had important advocates. In these years, however, certain scholars and teachers began a Shinto restoration movement to reinvigorate the faith. One such teacher was Munetada Kurozumi (1780–1850), to whom the story in the following selection is attributed. Kurozumi was born into a family of Shinto priests, and his teachings went on to become the basis of a new denomination of Shinto known as Kurozumikyo, which remains popular today as one of the post–World War II "new religions" of Japan. In the selection the teacher, known here by the name Kyoso, cures a sick person of his ills by prescribing laughter, since that will help him to follow the "divine way" of the Great Kami, who for Kyoso was the sun goddess Amaterasu.

Munetada Kurozumi, "The Benefits Realized Through Laughter," in *The Living Way: Stories of Kurozumi Munetada, a Shinto Founder*, narr. Tadaaki Kurozami and Isshi Kohmoto, trans. Sumio Kamiya, ed. Willis Stoesz. Walnut Creek, CA: Altamira Press, 1999. Copyright © 1999 by Willis Stoesz. Reproduced by permission of the publisher.

There was a sick person living in the city of Okayama who had been suffering a serious case of tuberculosis. Kyōso was invited to his place to perform a ritual of *majinai* [healing] on him. After the ritual Kyōso told him, "I am sorry to say it, but I have been thinking ever since I got here that this room is very gloomy. It is natural that your illness would have that result, and that your heart is gloomy with all your troubles and difficulties. And the members of your family also are in a gloomy and dark mood all the time. Furthermore, the doors and *shōji* screens are kept closed, making the room even darker. It is full of gloominess.

"Although your situation is understandable and reasonable, gloominess is taboo for one who is devoted in faith. Vitalizing your life is the divine way of things. Enjoying your life is the divine way, so practise complying with the holy heart of Great Kami. Please try to get a spark of cheerfulness into yourself. The first thing you should do is to laugh. It looks like you have not laughed for years. From this very day try to laugh as much and as often as possible."

The man replied, "Thank you, sir. But it is hard for me to laugh. I am not in a mood for it. How can I laugh?" Kyōso gave him this reply, "I can only say, 'Try to laugh. Do your best.' Although you have no reason to laugh you should try anyhow. You might just have to do it on purpose. Open your mouth wide open and say, 'ha, ha, ha.' I'm sure it will be easy for you. Give it a try."

All through the night the patient kept pondering this. "To laugh on purpose might not be so hard. I think I could do that. If it really would relieve me of my illness it would be an easy way to be cured." He started trying to laugh. But since he felt nothing to laugh at he found no joy in it. He thought how ridiculous it was even to try. With reluctance, again and again, he tried to laugh. "Ha, ha, ha."

Then he happened to notice that the paper-covered lantern was reflecting his shadow on the *fusuma* screen. His face was gaunt and rawboned, no flesh was left on his cheeks, and his mouth was moving in an awkward way as he seriously tried with all his might to laugh. It dawned on him how grotesque his shadow was looking. It was extremely funny! Suddenly he saw how comic it was! No one would be able to keep from laughing! It was an unexpected experience for him, after trying on purpose to laugh for no reason at all. Spontaneously he burst into real laughter. The humour was suddenly more than he could hold in. For some moments his sides were shaking with merriment.

The unusual sound woke up the members of his family and they came running to his room. The story and the funny shadow made them all laugh. Of course, the patient in turn was provoked to join them in even more laughter. Their sides were shaking as they were laughing, all of them.

The laughing he had not enjoyed for years relieved him of the congestion of blood in his stomach. His blood circulation showed sudden improvement. With his abdominal muscles activated, his appetite was enhanced and he began to feel hungry. Best of all, his gloominess all faded away and he felt happy and joyful. Although he ate only a little at his next meal he ate it with a hearty appetite. That night he sank into a deep and profound sleep such as he had been missing for years. His condition improved from the following morning on and eventually he was able to overcome the incurable disease.

It was indeed a blessing of *warai-harai*, "laughing-purification," because the patient was able to purify himself through laughter.

CHAPTER 3

State Shinto in the
Meiji Era and After,
1868–1945

Emperor Worship Becomes a Source of National Unity

by Peter Martin

Japan's long period of isolation under the Tokugawa shoguns came to an end in 1853 when American naval ships, under the command of Commodore Matthew Perry, arrived to insist that America be granted trade rights and other privileges. Similar missions from other Western powers followed, and Japanese leaders found themselves forced to open the country. Struggles between traditionalists and those who wanted to modernize Japan using Western models resulted in a brief civil war in 1867 after the death of the emperor Komei. The modernizers were victorious and in 1868 installed on the throne of Japan Mutsuhito, who came to be known as the Meiji emperor. Under Meiji and his two successors, Taisho and Showa, Japan not only modernized, it rose to great power. Japanese emperors are usually referred to by the name given their reign, thus Mutsuhito's rule covered the Meiji era from 1867 until his death in 1912. The reign names are granted postumously. Thus Hirohito, who ruled from 1926 to 1989, was only referred to as the Showa emperor after his death.

The new Meiji leaders, meanwhile, took advantage of the Shinto revival that began in the last half century of the Tokugawa era and used Shinto to unite the Japanese people and instill in them a sense of purpose

Peter Martin, *The Chrysanthemum Throne: A History of the Emperors of Japan.*
Honolulu: University of Hawaii Press, 1997. Copyright © 1997 by Peter Martin.
All rights reserved. Reproduced by permission of Sutton Publishing Ltd.

112

and destiny. Peter Martin, the author of the following selection, describes some of the major features of this process. Buddhist institutions were suppressed, Shinto departments of the national government were established, and Shinto festivals and ceremonies were given new emphasis. In addition, the emperor himself was declared to be divine and, as the author notes, ordinary people were expected to hold him in awe and reverence. Peter Martin served as a cultural counselor at the British embassy in Tokyo and has written a number of books. Under the pen name James Melville, he has published two historical novels set in Japan.

The doctrine that Japanese emperors were divine may in an important sense be said to have been invented in the 1880s at the instigation of the statesman Count Ito, on his return from a visit he made to Count Otto von Bismarck. As the 'Iron Chancellor' who had been the architect of German unification, Bismarck knew a thing or two about fostering a sense of national identity, and he imparted his conclusions on the subject to his eager Japanese visitor. 'Bismarck's advice was this,' the veteran politician Count Okuma told the American journalist Willard Smith in 1915. 'Revive those parts of Shinto that exalt the authority and divinity of the emperor.' Whatever the degree of authenticity of this anecdote, there is no doubt that this is precisely the course followed by the late nineteenth-century Japanese oligarchs.

Shinto and the myth of the origins of Japan had of course already been revived. They had, in fact, never been forgotten; and though it lacked an ideological framework, Shinto was a vital factor in the shaping of the [Meiji] restoration. A proclamation of 5 April 1868 announced that 'henceforth the government will be based on a return to the Imperial Rule of Jimmu Tenno [the supposed first emperor of Japan, circa the seventh century B.C.]'; and on 22 April in the following year imperial envoys were sent to venerate the supposed tomb of Jimmu, the founding emperor. Three days after that, the young Meiji himself, with senior members of his court and representatives of the *daimyos* [Japan's nobles], took part in a solemn ceremony to worship all the gods of the Shinto pantheon and swear allegiance to the charter oath [of 1868, expressing the ideals of the new regime]. This last was a short formulation of the aims and objectives of the new government, and had just been drawn up. In this first flush of enthusiasm a radical but doomed attempt was initiated to separate Shinto completely from the Buddhism with which it had become inextricably entwined over the centuries. Shinto priests who had simultaneously been in Buddhist orders were commanded to let their hair grow long as proof that they had renounced their affiliation with Buddhism. Buddhist priests who had, under the Tokugawa regime [1600–1868] been permitted to function as such in Shinto shrines were required either to return to secular life or to accept reordination as Shinto priests, in which case they were to start wearing Shinto vestments immediately. It was forbidden for the funeral services for these men or any member of their families to be conducted according to Buddhist rites. The pressure was maintained and even increased with the confiscation of all temple lands in February 1871, and the removal from the imperial palace precincts of all Buddhist statues and ritual objects and their transfer to a temple outside. This was accompanied by the abandonment of all the Buddhist ceremonies previously commissioned by the imperial household.

Targeting Buddhism

By the following year, the government had to accept that its policy of 'replacing' Buddhism by Shinto was causing serious social and political problems. Buddhism was deeply ingrained in the culture of Japan, and addressed itself to aspects of life which had not for well over a thousand years been regarded as the preserve of Shinto. Aggressive Christian missionaries made no secret of their hope that their own creed would replace Buddhism. The anti-Buddhist ordinances created more problems than they solved at almost every level, and were therefore quietly shelved for a decade. When Shinto was in the 1880s once again promoted by the authorities it was in a new, subtler guise: that of all-embracing emperor worship.

The forging of a national consciousness among people who had—particularly in the domains of the 'outsider lords'—a generation earlier thought of themselves as owing allegiance to their local *daimyo*, rather than to an emperor of whom the vast majority had possibly never heard, was going quite well. There were problems, of course. The architects of the Meiji restoration were not always of one mind, and the 1870s saw a number of attempts on the part of disgruntled individuals to challenge the policies of the new government.

The most serious of these was an armed rebellion led by a founding member of the oligarchy itself. He was a senior samurai [Japan's elite warrior class] from Satsuma called Saigo Takamori. Saigo was charismatic but

vain; an opinionated and ambitious man who decorated his house with portraits of Napoleon I and III,
Frederick the Great and Charlemagne. Collegiate government was never to his taste, and, when his recom-
mendation that an invasion of Korea should be
mounted was rejected by his colleagues, he resigned
and exiled himself to Kyushu, where he waited in vain
to be recalled to save the nation. In 1877 he was persuaded by some of his more romantic supporters there
to take up arms against the Tokyo government. Against
his own better judgement, and virtually disabled by
kidney stones (like his hero Napoleon III [emperor of
France 1852–1870]), Saigo led a small army of disaf-
fected samurai into battle at Kumamoto Castle. There
he and his men were decisively defeated by government troops, and Saigo with a handful of his most loyal
lieutenants retreated in disorder to the outskirts of the
city of Kagoshima far to the south, where he protested
his loyalty to the emperor Meiji and committed *seppuku* [ritual suicide].

The taste for heroic failure which has always charac-
terised the Japanese ensured that Saigo was posthumously rehabilitated, and a statue of him in informal
Japanese dress, attended by his much-loved dog, today
occupies a prominent site in Ueno Park in Tokyo. But
all the same he lost. During the civil wars of the fifteenth and sixteenth centuries a cynical catchphrase
was current: *kateba kangun* ('whichever side wins is the
imperial army'). The humiliating defeat of Saigo emp-
tied the phrase of meaning. Just a decade after the
restoration, Japan now had but one modern national
army, and though led by officers of samurai birth, it
consisted in the main of peasant conscripts who had
waged effective war in the name of their emperor.

State Shinto

A new, national patriotism had been born. Nevertheless, it was thought necessary for the people to be provided with an ideological framework which would reinforce their loyalty. Accordingly a new cult, which was designated State Shinto, was established at the behest of the Tokyo government. Ito and his associates and their staff resuscitated the mythology recounted by the court chroniclers of the eighth century and repeated by the Mito School [proponents of the centrality of the emperor] a thousand years later. On their instructions, scholars and chamberlains investigated and codified in the minutest detail the ancient rituals relating to the throne and the sacerdotal duties of its occupant, the knowledge of which had been transmitted mainly through oral tradition and which had been revived sporadically since the civil strife of the fourteenth, fifteenth and sixteenth centuries. They added an extra dash of Confucianism, and tricked the mixture out to suit the exigencies of the time, much as King George V [of Great Britain] and his courtiers, in an attempt to 'keep the twentieth century at bay' were to reinvent the monarchy in Britain after the death of Edward VII.

Shinto priests were given salaries as minor civil servants, and for the first time were legally authorised to conduct marriage and funeral ceremonies. Buddhism, which had been patronised and promoted for more than twelve hundred years by emperors who routinely entered Buddhist orders after abdication and nominated their sons and daughters as abbots and nuns, was again forced to surrender some traditional privileges. In an extraordinarily short time the brand new Shinto wedding ceremony became the norm, and remains so throughout Japan. The consolations of Buddhism, however, continued to be sought by those in distress; virtually all funerals are still conducted according to its rites.

The emperor Meiji now disappeared from the view of the ordinary man and woman in the street, but in an abstract sense was omnipresent. The common people were required to hold in reverent awe a sovereign they were never permitted to set eyes on. When his closed carriage passed through the streets, all upper windows had to be shuttered so that nobody could look down from above on the vehicle containing his sacred person; and even those few courtiers and high officials permitted to enter his presence never raised their eyes to his. His clothes did not fit him very well, because no tailor could presume to run a tape measure over the physical manifestation of a living god, which was off-limits even to his physicians.

Revering the Emperor

On the other hand, his photograph was the most venerated object in every school in the land. It was ritually displayed several times each year, when the Imperial Rescript on Education of 1890 was read aloud. This same rescript was hurriedly given a new but strictly temporary lease of life in late 1945 by Prince Higashikuni, Japan's first postwar prime minister, who with other members of the pre-war establishment put up a dogged but doomed rearguard action to keep it in force. It was well described by W.K. Bunce, one of General [Douglas] MacArthur's senior civilian advisers [during the post–World War II American occupation of Japan], as '. . . a Shinto-Confucianist document written for the purpose of keeping down "radical" (i.e. democratic) tendencies . . .'. The official English translation published at the time of its original promulgation ran as follows:

> Our Imperial Ancestors have founded our Empire on a basis broad and everlasting. Our subjects ever united in loyalty and filial piety have from generation to generation illustrated the beauty thereof. This is the glory of the fundamental character of Our Empire, and herein also lies the source of Our Education. Ye, Our Subjects, be filial to your parents, affectionate to your brothers and sisters; as husbands and wives be harmonious; as friends, true. Pursue learning and cultivate arts, and thereby develop intellectual faculties and perfect moral powers; furthermore, advance public good and promote common interests; always respect the Constitution and observe the laws; should emergency arise, offer yourselves courageously to the State; and thus guard and maintain the prosperity of Our Imperial Throne coeval with heaven and earth. So shall ye be not only Our good and faithful subjects, but render illustrious the best traditions of your forefathers. The Way here set forth is indeed the teaching bequeathed by Our Imperial Ancestors, to be observed alike by Their Descendants and the subjects, infallible for all ages and true in all places. It is Our wish to lay it to heart in all reverence, in common with you, Our subjects, that we may all thus attain to the same virtue.

The remarkable new cult of State Shinto was, designedly, never officially described as a religion, and was to endure for less than sixty years. Nevertheless, during that period it flourished mightily, and many westerners assume it to have ancient origins on that account. In terms of western logic and theology it was full of gaping holes. It was never clearly stated at what precise moment emperors became divine. Certainly not through the *Daijosai* [coronation] ritual, which sometimes took place several years after the installation of a new incumbent on the throne. Nor was the status in Shinto terms of a crown prince or even a prince re-

Here Hirohito wears imperial robes and the distinctive headdress of a Shinto priest.

gent ever defined. During the years of Meiji's 'divinity', his son the future emperor Taisho appeared in public from time to time, and though his rank ensured that he was treated with enormous respect, until he succeeded his father it was never suggested that he was other than fully human. By the same token, during Taisho's own reign, divinity was never claimed for his son and heir Prince Hirohito. Even as prince regent he went about freely and was once photographed in the company of the visiting Prince of Wales in golfing attire complete with jaunty flat cap.

The awkward historical fact that so many past emperors had in their lifetimes become Buddhist priests was never explained or even referred to, and there cannot be much doubt that, however devoted they were to their sovereign, few intelligent Japanese were seriously deceived by the astonishing theories they had to pretend to swallow. Nevertheless, when he died, in the age of the motor car and the aeroplane, Meiji was mourned as a god, and his spirit is now enshrined in the huge Shinto complex erected in Tokyo to commemorate his reign, alongside that of his empress Shoken, who died two years after her husband and was the only Japanese woman ever to be officially apotheosised [made divine].

Whether or not Meiji himself was persuaded that he had, over a short period in the middle of his life, ceased to be a normal human being and become a god, he dutifully behaved in the manner deemed appropriate to his new role, and earned in political terms the status of father figure to his people.

Shinto Is the Basis of Our National Life

by Genchi Kato

The following selection comes from a pamphlet entitled *What Is Shinto?* It was written by a Japanese scholar for foreign travelers to his country, part of a collection of travel pamphlets assembled by the Japanese tourist board. Published in 1935, it makes clear the government's emphasis on state Shinto as the focus for national unity. The author, Genchi Kato, notes that there are thirteen Shinto sects whose emphasis is on religious matters: prayer and ritual to the *kami*, or gods. But above that is state Shinto, which gives a religious quality to national life and reveres the emperor as divine. The selection is therefore a good example of the increasingly strident nationalist rhetoric used by Japanese leaders and their spokesmen as World War II approached. Particularly telling is the author's claim that Buddhism and Confucianism, both central to any understanding of Japanese culture and history, are "alien teachings." Genchi Kato was the author of many books on Shinto, including *A Study of Shinto: The Religion of the Japanese Nation.* He taught at the Tokyo Imperial University and headed the Meiji Japan Society. American occupation officials removed him from these positions in 1945 on the grounds that he represented militaristic nationalism.

Genchi Kato, *What Is Shinto?* Tokyo: Maruzen Company Ltd., 1935.

Shintō at present may be divided into two classes: Sectarian or Denominational Shintō consisting of thirteen sects, and the National Shintō Faith of the Japanese people, very often called State Shintō to distinguish it from the thirteen sects of Shintō or Denominational Shintō. The National Shintō Faith makes its manifestation in the form of the so-called "Jinja Shintō," that is to say, the Shintō symbolized by means of a shrine structure, while it is taught in schools to the younger generation under the name of Japanese national ethics. Now, Shintō, as the national faith of Japan, has developed into a unique form of Japanese morality, glowing with the holy fire of religion, and just herein lies the peculiar Japanese patriotism or loyalty to the Akitsu Kami or Divine Ruler—that Japanese loyalty which is suffused with a "devotional quality of religious intensity." Shintō, as the national faith, is the essentially guiding principle, both ethical and religious, on which its national life has been firmly and fundamentally established.

From what is said above, it can be easily and clearly seen that Shintō, whether Sectarian or National, is not a dead religion like that of bygone Greece or Rome, but, has a vitality in no way inferior to that of Buddhism, Christianity or Islam. It is the religion which, flourishing in Japan from ancient times, maintains its vigour today unabated. It is true that Shintō has been influenced to a great extent by alien teachings of Buddhism and Confucianism for instance, yet it has never been annihilated by imported foreign creeds. On the contrary, it has unfailingly maintained itself, generation after generation, revealing from time to time new phases of a higher and higher order of religion. The national

religion of ancient Greece has long ceased to be, as
[seventeenth-century English poet John] Milton once
happily sang:

Apollo from his shrine
Can no more divine,
With hollow shriek the steep of
Delphos leaving.

The national religion of early Rome has shared the
same sad fate. The religion of ancient Egypt, the old religions of Babylonia and Assyria have passed into obliv-
ion. All these religions are things of the past, gone forever, representing no faith of peoples of today. It is
quite otherwise with Shintō. Every one of the thirteen
Shintō sects has large numbers of professed believers,
while the National Shintō Faith stands as one of the
fundamental spiritual characteristics of the Japanese
people. Every year the Ise Shrine attracts hundreds of
thousands of devout pilgrims to pay homage to the Ancestral Sun-Goddess; while Shintō shrines with their
picturesque red-coloured gateways in front, dotted
everywhere throughout the length and breadth of the
land, are objects of veneration and worship, eloquently
testifying that Shintō endures as a national faith. In Europe, a world religion, Christianity, has replaced or dis-
placed the older national faiths of Greece and Rome. In
Japan, however, the national Shintō religion has never
been superseded by any universal religion, either Buddhism or Christianity, imported into the Island Empire.
Just herein lies one of the fundamental characteristics
of the religious history of Japan.

As War Approached, Japanese Leaders Demanded More of Shinto Shrines

by Koremaru Sakamoto

Even though the Meiji leaders of Japan, a coalition of traditional aristocrats, industrialists, and military officers, used Shinto to foment national unity, they never proclaimed officially that their state Shinto was a religion and asserted furthermore that Japan was a nation of complete religious freedom. This created confusion among believers and, as scholar Koremaru Sakamoto writes in the following selection, placed Shinto shrines in an especially difficult position, with priests never quite sure whether they were serving the state or serving the *kami* (gods).

These problems grew especially acute as Japan's territorial ambitions exploded into large-scale war. Already in possession of Korea and Taiwan, Japan invaded Manchuria, north of China, in 1931, and after its victory established a puppet state there. In 1937 Japan invaded China itself, and World War II in Asia had begun. With Japan on a war footing, leaders believed it was now necessary for Shinto shrines to serve even more than before as a focus of patriotism. As Sakamoto indi-

Koremaru Sakamoto, "The Structure of State Shinto: Its Creation, Development, and Demise," in *Shinto in History: Ways of the Kami,* ed. John Breen and Mark Teeuwen. Honolulu: University of Hawaii Press, 2000. Copyright © 2000 by John Breen and Mark Teeuwen. Reproduced by permission of Taylor & Francis Group Ltd.

cates, they established a government office known as Jingiin to reinforce faith in the divinity of the emperor. Koremaru Sakamoto is professor of Shinto studies at Kokugakuin Daigaku, the Shinto university in Tokyo.

The funeral of the Taishō emperor [Yoshihito, reigned 1912–1926], the enthronement rites of the Shōwa emperor, [Hirohito, reigned 1926–1989] and the ritual rebuilding of the Ise shrines [in 1929] were all state rites and ceremonies intimately related to the ideal of venerating the deities. They played their part in spreading that ideal throughout Japan. Shrine visits had now become established practice at primary school; there was a growing sense that refusal to visit a shrine disqualified one as a citizen of the imperial nation. This tendency was given added impetus when, with the outbreak of the so-called Manchurian incident in 1931 [a Japanese invasion of Manchuria, north of China], it became customary practice to pray for victory at shrines. This was precisely why the government was in dread lest shrines seek to enhance their religious qualities, and lest there appear, from among the people, an insistence that shrines were, after all, religious. The Meiji constitution [of 1889] had made no provision for a state religion; it sought rather to adhere to the basic principle that, as long as there was no compromise of a citizen's duties and no threat to social order, a diversity of religious belief was permissible. [Scholar] Akazawa Shirō argues that 'shrines assumed a sudden prominence' on account of the fact that 'in state Shinto universalistic norms transcending the state, capable of passing judgement on the state, did not exist, and this led to the absolute legitimation of war as an act of state; but if this had been the case, it would surely have been possible for the government, in a fascist sort of way, to enforce shrine worship and allow no space for debates over the religious quality or otherwise of shrines. However, even in the midst of the Manchurian incident, 'one of those absolutely legitimised acts of state', the government was still struggling with the issue of the nature, religious or not, of shrines. At a special meeting of the Shrine Commission on December 21, 1931, [leading politician] Egi Kazutoshi made the following speech:

> At our previous meeting, [politician] Mizuno [Rentaro] spoke about some religious person or other who insisted that religious activity at shrines be stopped. This person argued that if shrines are seen as non-religious, then all religious activity at shrines should be done away with. Such opinions are gaining ground. There was the view expressed that it would be appropriate to consider this matter. This is, indeed, a most reasonable view and, at our earlier meeting, frequent reference was made to it. We have not as yet, it is true, devoted our deliberations exclusively to this problem. The opening of the next session of the Diet [parliament] is imminent. When the Diet reconvenes, I am sure that questions will be raised. The government must address itself to this problem. The Commission must consider its position carefully, and it would, of course, be splendid if the wishes of the Commission coincided with those of government. In any case, it is surely imperative that this whole question is given the most careful consideration in the Diet.

In other words, for the government, the question of the non-religious quality of shrines still constituted a major problem. Of course, in the background was the perennial, unresolved matter of the standardised administration and control of religions under a religious law, which reached back to the 1890s. For the government of the time, *the* issue was how to mobilise the people for a quasi-war footing. Given that this was so, the state's ability to control the world of religion, with its organisational and mobilising capability vastly superior to that of shrines alone, was an issue upon which, at the risk of some exaggeration, the very survival of the state was seen to depend. The state's greatest challenge, therefore, was to create a structure that would facilitate the mobilisation of *all* religions in support of state policy; one which would, in turn, ensure that the ideal of reverence for the deities was sustained without causing friction with other religions. For that reason, too, the government had no choice but to work feverishly to embrace other religious groups. At this juncture, the state did not have the capacity, the 'fascist capacity' if you will, to force on the entire religious world shrine worship and, through it, reverence for the deities.

Religious Support for War

All the government and Home Ministry could do was insist that shrines were not religious and that 'compulsory' attendance at shrines was not in breach of religious freedom. It goes without saying that compulsion expressed in these defensive terms was quite lacking in force. On September 22, 1934, the Catholic Archbishop of Tokyo asked the Education Ministry about students' and pupils' shrine veneration. The Ministry responded to the inquiry a week or so later: 'The attendance of students, children and pupils at shrines is required for educational purposes. The respect required of such groups is quite simply a sign of patriotism and loyalty.' It is plain enough from this statement that, for government, shrines were nothing more than the objects of 'respect'. It is all too easy to imagine how such a view of shrines dampened their vitality. It is not at all surprising that provincial Shintoists and others disposed to a genuine reverence for enshrined deities attacked such views; nor that many people rushed to join Shinto-type religious groups or other similar religious bodies. The logic of the Home Ministry was that shrine attendance could be enforced since shrines were not religious, but were simply to be respected for reasons of 'national ethics'. This could never lead to more than a superficial concern for the nation's shrines. This government logic was persuasive only to faithless ritualists and modern rational bureaucrats, for whom shrines were on a par with the flag and the national anthem.

So the government sought the restructuring of the shrine system alone, but even this it did not set about with special enthusiasm. The Shrine Commission, too, gave up arguing about thorny issues and buried its head in secular institutional concerns. Indecisive arguments endured ad infinitum; and the Commission was capable of not much more than making a show of submitting petitions to government, which the Diet itself had anyway submitted ages before. So, for example, the Commission petitioned the government in November 1936 to give urgent attention to the creation of an office dedicated to deity affairs. The government's organisation of the shrine system proceeded in parallel with a whole train of events that were suggestive of a semi-war footing in Japan. I refer to the Manchurian incident in 1931, the establishment of Manchukuo [the Japanese puppet state in Manchuria] in March 1932, Japan's departure from the League of Nations in 1933, the expanding *kokutai meichō* or 'clarification of the national polity' movement that originated in opposition to the Emperor Organ theory controversy in 1935 [a legal controversy over a claim that the emperor was only an "organ" of the state]. The February 26th incident in 1936 [a military mutiny] and the Sino-Japanese war of 1937. In these extreme circumstances, the movement to achieve national unity on the basis of ideas rooted in the national polity gathered increasing strength and momentum. Actions, words and thoughts which cut across these ideals were suppressed and controlled by means of a range of laws, such as the Law Against Subversive Actions and the Peace Preservation Law. The attempts to enforce national solidarity by means of various 'security measures' were, in terms of their character, quite some distance removed from religion. The government thought its best bet was to command and control the broad framework of regulated religions and religious groups by setting up an integrated religious law; and to regulate anything that escaped that framework with the Peace Preservation Law. In other words, it sought to lay out a system in which religious law was the carrot and the Peace Preservation Law the stick with which religions might be controlled and mobilised.

The government's desire for the invigoration of security laws and for the creation of a law on religions intensified as Japan sank deeper into the mire of the Sino-Japanese war. The strong pull of government toward the latter was, needless to say, inseparable from any restructuring and filling out of the shrine system. The ZSK [*Zenkoku Shinsho Kukai*, or National Association for Shrine Priests] for its part worked relentlessly on government and Diet for improvements to shrines and the creation of a dedicated organ of government for deity affairs. New impetus was added to these moves with the formation in January of 1939 of a new government by Hiranuma Ki'ichirō (1867–1952). Hiranuma's cabinet came to power with promises to invigorate the national spirit and revamp education; the cabinet's approach to shrines was also a positive one. On February 25th, Home Minister Kido Kōichi (1889–1977) fielded a question by [Diet member] Senshū Suetaka (1875–1941) at a budgetary sub-committee meeting on the issue of the long sought-after government office for deity affairs. Kido said in reply that he hoped such an office might see fruition not long after the start of the following financial year. Hiranuma himself concurred with this view. The Hiranuma cabinet's positive approach ensured swift moves in the direction of shrine system restructuring, and the Home Ministry's *Jinjakyoku* [Shrine Bureau], which since 1933 had been gradually reformed, witnessed a rapid strengthening and a marked diversification in responsibility. Noteworthy among the reforms now implemented was the creation of two new sections, for 'Instruction' and 'Building', and new ranks and a higher status for incumbents. With the Sino-Japanese war dragging on, the question of maintaining and expanding the network of shrines dedicated to the war dead surfaced as a pressing problem. In March, such shrines were restyled *gokoku jinja* ('nation-protecting shrines'), and the whole network of such shrines, fragile till now, was rapidly reinforced.

Bureaucracy and 'Nation-Protecting Shrines'

Such was the state of affairs in 1940, the 2,600th anniversary of the founding of the imperial line. The entire nation was simmering with a mood of celebration; and there was a grandness about the way in which, say, ex-

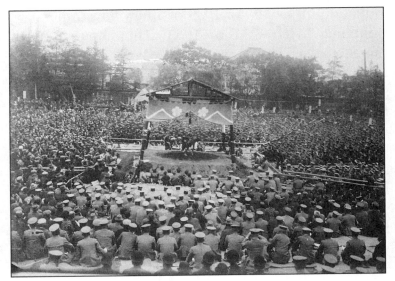

During World War II, Japanese soldiers watch wrestling matches at Tokyo's Yasukuni shrine, a shrine dedicated to Japan's war dead.

tension works were carried out to the Kashihara shrine in Nara, dedicated to the (mythical) first Emperor Jinmu (also known as Jimmu Tenno), and likewise to the creation of the Ōmi shrine in Ōtsu, where the 7th century Emperor Tenchi is venerated. The cabinet, now under Prime Minister Konoe Fumimaro (1891–1945), decided finally to commit itself to setting up a dedicated office of state for 'deity affairs', and the emperor was asked to approve its being named the *Jingiin* in October. The Privy Council deliberated the cabinet proposal, and formed a special committee to give it the closest inspection at the end of the month. At the committee's first meeting, Home Minister Yasui Eiji (1890–1982) explained the idea behind the proposal and then took questions. What is especially interesting here is the Home Minister's view that the *Jingiin* would not be an organ charged with direct supervision of ritual; it would rather concern itself with perfecting the shrine network. There was a major question here concerning the emperor's supreme authority over ritual matters, of course, and committee member Shimizu Tōru (1868–1947) inquired about the 'unifying of state ritual and court ritual', but the only response forthcoming was from Iinuma Kazumi (1892–1982) who ran the *Jinjakyoku*. He agreed the question merited 'due consideration'. The committee approved unanimously the original proposal, and committee chairman, Arima Ryōkitsu (1861–1944), formally advised the Privy Council to approve the creation of the *Jingiin*. . . .

The birth of the *Jingiin* marked the first time that government had ever officially added its weight to the dissemination of a political ideology rooted in the ideal of reverence for the deities. For the first time, that is, ideology had been implanted in what had been 'state Shinto' in purely institutional terms.

The Shinto Directive of 1945

by General Headquarters of the Supreme Commander for the Allied Powers, Tokyo

World War II in Asia began with Japan's 1937 invasion of China, followed in 1940 and 1941 by Japanese occupation of Vietnam, Malaysia, Singapore, and Indonesia, at that time all colonies of various European countries. America entered the war when Japan, seeking to forestall any American threat to their ambitions, bombed the U.S. naval base at Pearl Harbor in Hawaii on December 7, 1941. Over the next four years the United States led the coalition that ultimately defeated Japan. The war ended with atomic bombs being dropped on the cities of Hiroshima and Nagasaki in August 1945. Stepping in when his government and military could not decide what to do, the Showa emperor of Japan, Hirohito, agreed to an unconditional surrender. He announced his decision over the radio on August 15. It was the first time most Japanese people had heard the voice of their allegedly divine emperor, and his announcement was followed by the ritual suicide, or seppuku, of many people on the grounds of the imperial palace in Tokyo.

American authorities occupied Japan for the next seven years, trying to reconstruct a nation that would

General Headquarters of the Supreme Commander for the Allied Powers, Tokyo, *The Shinto Directive*, 1945.

remain peaceful and reject the nationalist excesses that had led to World War II. Among their first efforts was to dismantle state Shinto, which they did with the Shinto Directive, the following selection. The directive separated Shinto institutions from the government and banned the publications and organizations that reinforced the notions that Shinto was the source of Japanese national life and that the Japanese were superior to other peoples. Hirohito, for his part, enjoyed a good working relationship with General Douglas MacArthur, the U.S. occupation commander. He announced formally and conclusively in 1947 that neither he nor any other Japanese emperor was a god as state Shinto had preached.

---

1. In order to free the Japanese people from direct or indirect compulsion to believe or profess to believe in a religion or cult officially designated by the state, and

In order to lift from the Japanese people the burden of compulsory financial support of an ideology which has contributed to their war guilt, defeat, suffering, privation, and present deplorable condition, and

In order to prevent a recurrence of the perversion of Shintō theory and beliefs into militaristic and ultranationalistic propaganda designed to delude the Japanese people and lead them into wars of aggression, and

In order to assist the Japanese people in a rededication of their national life to building a new Japan based upon ideals of perpetual peace and democracy,

It is hereby dictated that:

a. The sponsorship, support, perpetuation, control and dissemination of Shintō by the Japanese national, prefectural, and local governments, or by public officials, subordinates, and employees acting in their official capacity are prohibited and will cease immediately.

b. All financial support from public funds and all official affiliation with Shintō and Shintō shrines are prohibited and will cease immediately.

(1) While no financial support from public funds will be extended to shrines located on public reservations or parks, this prohibition will not be construed to preclude the Japanese government from continuing to support the areas on which such shrines are located.

(2) Private financial support of all Shintō shrines which have been previously supported in whole or in part by public funds will be permitted, provided such private support is entirely voluntary and is in no way derived from forced or involuntary contributions.

c. All propagation and dissemination of militaristic and ultranationalistic ideology in Shintō doctrines, practices, rites, ceremonies, or observances, as well as in the doctrines, practices, rites, ceremonies, and observances of any other religion, sect, creed, or philosophy, are prohibited and will cease immediately.

d. The Religious Functions Order relating to the Grand Shrine of Ise and the Religious Functions Order relating to State and other Shrines will be annulled.

e. The Shrine Board (*Jingi-in*) of the Ministry of Home Affairs will be abolished, and its present functions, duties, and administrative obligations will not be assumed by any other governmental or tax-supported agency.

f. All public educational institutions whose primary function is either the investigation and dissemination of Shintō or the training of a Shintō priesthood will be abolished and their physical properties diverted to other uses. Their present function, duties and administrative obligations will not be assumed by any other governmental or tax-supported agency.

g. Private educational institutions for the investigation and dissemination of Shintō and for the training of priesthood will be permitted and will operate with the same privileges and be subject to the same controls and restrictions as any other private educational institution having no affiliation with the government; in no case, however, will they receive support from public funds, and in no case will they propagate and disseminate militaristic and ultranationalistic ideology.

h. The dissemination of Shintō doctrines in any form and by any means in any educational institution supported wholly or in part by public funds is prohibited and will cease immediately.

(1) All teachers' manuals and textbooks now in use in any educational institution supported wholly or in part by public funds will be censored, and all Shintō doctrine will be deleted. No teachers' manual or textbook which is published in the future for use in such institutions will contain any Shintō doctrine.

(2) No visits to Shintō shrines and no rites, practices or ceremonies associated with Shintō will be conducted or sponsored by any educational institution supported wholly or in part by public funds.

i. Circulation by the government of *The Fundamental Principles of the National Structure (Kokutai no Hongi), The Way of the Subject (Shinmin no Michi)*, and all similar official volumes, commentaries, interpretations, or instructions on Shintō are prohibited.

j. The use in official writings of the terms "Greater East Asia War" (*Dai Tōn Sensō*), "The Whole World Under One Roof" (*Hakko Ichi-u*), and all other terms whose connotation in Japanese is inextricably connected with

State Shintō, militarism, and ultranationalism is prohibited and will cease immediately.

k. God-shelves (*Kamidana*) and all other physical symbols of State Shintō in any office, school, institution, organization, or structure supported wholly or in part by public funds are prohibited and will be removed immediately.

l. No official, subordinate, employee, student, citizen, or resident of Japan will be discriminated against because of his failure to profess and believe in or participate in any practice, rite, ceremony, or observance of State Shintō or any other religion.

m. No official of the national, prefectural, or local government, acting in his public capacity, will visit any shrine to report his assumption of office, to report on conditions of government or to participate as a representative of government in any ceremony or observance.

2. a. The purpose of this directive is to separate religion from the state, to prevent misuse of religion for political ends, and to put all religions, faiths, and creeds upon exactly the same basis, entitled to precisely the same opportunities and protection. It forbids affiliation with the government and the propagation and dissemination of militaristic and ultranationalistic ideology not only to Shintō but to the followers of all religions, faiths, sects, creeds, or philosophies.

b. The provisions of this directive will apply with equal force to all rites, practices, ceremonies, observances, beliefs, teachings, mythology, legends, philosophy, shrines, and physical symbols associated with Shintō.

c. The term State Shintō within the meaning of this directive will refer to that branch of Shintō (*Kokka Shintō* or *Jinja Shintō*) which by official acts of the Japanese Government has been differentiated from the religion of Sect Shintō (*Shūha Shintō*) and has been classified a non-religious cult commonly known as State Shintō, National Shintō, or Shrine Shintō.

d. The term Sect Shintō (*Shūha Shintō* or *Kyōha Shintō*) will refer to that branch of Shintō (composed of 13 recognized sects) which by popular belief, legal commentary, and the official acts of the Japanese Government has been recognized to be a religion.

e. Pursuant to the terms of Article 1 of the Basic Directive on "Removal of Restrictions on Political, Civil, and Religious Liberties" issued on 4 October 1945 by the Supreme Commander for the Allied Powers in which the Japanese people were assured complete religious freedom.

(1) Sect Shintō will enjoy the same protection as any other religion.

(2) Shrine Shintō, after having been divorced from the state and divested of its militaristic and ultranationalistic elements, will be recognized as a religion if its adherents so desire and will be granted the same protection as any other religion in so far as it may in fact be the philosophy or religion of Japanese individuals.

f. Militaristic and ultranationalistic ideology, as used in this directive, embraces those teachings, beliefs, and theories which advocate or justify a mission on the part of Japan to extend its rule over other nations and peoples by reason of:

(1) The doctrine that the Emperor of Japan is superior to the heads of other states because of ancestry, descent, or special origin.

(2) The doctrine that the people of Japan are superior to the people of other lands because of ancestry, descent, or special origin.

(3) The doctrine that the islands of Japan are superior

to other lands because of divine or special origin.

(4) Any other doctrine which tends to delude the Japanese people into embarking upon wars of aggression or to glorify the use of force as an instrument for the settlement of disputes with other peoples.

3. The Imperial Japanese Government will submit a comprehensive report to this Headquarters not later than 15 March 1946 describing in detail all action taken to comply with all provisions of this directive.

4. All officials, subordinates, and employees of the Japanese national, prefectural, and local governments, all teachers and education officials, and all citizens and residents of Japan will be held personally accountable for compliance with the spirit as well as the letter of all provisions of this directive.

CHAPTER 4

Shinto in Modern Times

The Three Modern Forms of Shinto

by William Horsley and Roger Buckley

Although Shinto worship is often based on common rituals, such as those concerned with purification, and certain Shinto *kami*, or gods, have become predominant, organized Shinto has been extremely amorphous. Sects have come and gone, and there are literally thousands of forms of worship. During the Meiji era, for instance (1868–1912), authorities claimed that not only were there thirteen Shinto sects focused on spirituality but also state Shinto, a separate line of thinking, which posited the divinity of the emperor and the unique nature of the Japanese people. After American occupation officials ended state Shinto in the years following World War II, Shinto lost its official state sponsorship and returned to a devotional focus.

According to William Horsley and Roger Buckley, the authors of the following selection, organized Shinto can be best understood in the modern era by dividing it into three main categories: the worship of local or family guardian gods; shrine Shinto, or popular worship; and the formal Shinto associated with the emperor and his court. The authors also contrast certain Shinto beliefs with certain Christian ones and note the lingering influences of Confucianism and Buddhism. William Hors-

William Horsley and Roger Buckley, *Nippon, New Superpower: Japan Since 1945.* London: BBC Books, 1990. Copyright © 1990 by William Horsley and Roger Buckley. Reproduced by permission.

ley and Roger Buckley are British reporters with long experience in Japan. The book from which this selection comes is a companion to the British Broadcasting Corporation's television series on modern Japan.

Shinto has three main strands, each of which is active today. Firstly it celebrates local clan spirits, originally called *ujigami*. These give expression to the idea of patriarchy: the clan (*uji*) and household are themselves seen as sacred institutions, and the ancestors—the departed heads of households—are venerated. The shrine complex at Nikko, Japan's most visited tourist spot, was built in honour of the *kami* enshrined there—none other than the first Tokugawa *shogun* [military ruler] Ieyasu, who first unified the whole country at the turn of the seventeenth century.

Secondly, there is shrine Shinto, the folk aspect of the religion, which blesses local communities through their Shinto observances. Shrine festivals, *matsuri*, are usually held twice each year, at the transplanting of the rice in spring and at harvest time in autumn; they have always represented an important focus of Japanese community life. Festivals are often a mixture of Shinto and Buddhist traditions, but above all they celebrate the cycle of the seasons and the fertility of nature. The highlight of the main festivals in autumn is the parading of the *mikoshi*—portable shrine—through the streets of the local area: at the time of the *matsuri* the local guardian god is supposed to move from the shrine building itself into a small, portable shrine kept in the precincts. This is a finely carved and decorated wooden miniature house, designed for the god to inhabit temporarily, which is held aloft on a pair of fixed poles. Young and old people of the community boisterously parade the *mikoshi* around out of doors, symbolically allowing the local guardian god to greet and mingle with the people.

Thirdly, there is court Shinto, which ascribes to the Emperor the role of the supreme high priest. It also identifies Shinto unmistakably as an ethnic creed: the Emperor is seen as the head of the nation-family, and as the chief *kami* of the whole population. A host of Shinto court rituals continue throughout the year.

Shinto, Christianity, and Confucianism

Whereas in Christianity man began in a state of innocence in the Garden of Eden and fell from grace, condemned to labour for his daily bread, in Japanese thought and literature there is no such Fall. Man is essentially innocent, and work has traditionally been seen not as a hardship but as a positive, life-asserting activity. The Christian concept of original sin is also absent from Japanese philosophical thought. On the contrary, the concept of 'original virtue', derived from Confucian thought, supports the Japanese assumption that men, and especially rulers or high-ranking people, are inherently virtuous. This idea was actively encouraged by the *shogun* in the Tokugawa period to bolster their own authority.

Rather than the concept of sin, the Japanese set important store by ritual purification. Thus at the approach to Shinto shrines worshippers customarily wash their hands in a stream, and at New Year households place small mounds of pure salt outside the threshold. Ground-breaking ceremonies held at the start of construction work, or before any organised endeavour, entail the exorcism of bad spirits by a priest waving a branch of the sakaki tree, which is deemed sacred, over the heads of the persons concerned.

Parallel in importance to the idea of ritual purification is the concept of pure intentions, or sincerity: *makoto*, which stems from both Shinto and Confucianist thinking, and is also consistent with the Buddhist idea of spiritual enlightenment. The stress on sincerity, in family and personal dealings and especially in relation to those in authority, has been reinforced and refined by centuries of Japanese living. In the Middle Ages, an age of shifting alliances and civil wars in Japan, this concept of inner purity of thought and action came to be upheld as a high ideal. It was closely connected to the concept of loyalty on the part of retainers to their feudal lords. Any allegiance to abstract or universal values not related to the social obligations of the present was strongly discouraged by the shogunate.

Despite Formal Rules, Shinto Followers Worship in Their Own Ways

by John K. Nelson

There are differences between formal Shinto and individual worship, as scholar of Shinto John K. Nelson makes clear in the following selection from his book *Enduring Identities: The Guise of Shinto in Contemporary Japan.* Although Shinto priests are trained in proper procedures, ordinary believers tend to follow their own variations of these procedures. These methods of personal worship, as the author suggests, reflect the fact that believers commonly worship in order to gain solace or comfort, or to seek help of some kind. They also, however, show that Shinto is an open and flexible faith, far less bound by strict rules, commandments, prescribed rites, and expectations than other major world religions. John K. Nelson teaches anthropology and religion at the University of Texas. His other books include *A Year in the Life of a Shinto Shrine.*

According to the priests, who are schooled in ritual propriety and must demonstrate their expertise before they can be promoted, a "correct" shrine visit includes a certain approach, an act of worship before the *kami*, and a prescribed departure. Regardless of the size of the shrine or its location in Japan, the first stage of this process still begins with an act emblematic of a great number of Shinto's ritual concerns: a purification at the stone water basin, the *temizusha*. The water is used to cleanse hands (symbolizing one's deeds and actions) and mouth (words) before one proceeds.

The Priests' Course

Following the Kamigamo [shrine] priests' course, one should then cross the Negi Bridge (thus attaining an automatic purification, since traversing flowing water extracts impurities) and pay one's respects before the shrine of Tamayorihime, the mythical mother of the principal deity. One then crosses the final bridge (another instant purification) before entering the Tower Gate, climbing the stone stairs, and finally arriving at the Middle Gate (Chūmon). Here, while looking into the splendidly preserved inner sanctuary compound that is shielded from full view by sedge-grass screens, curtains, and low eaves, one might compose one's prayer or petition. Then, after tossing in a few coins (ideally, the priests say, one hundred yen) that serve as donations and as another way to cast out impurities, one enacts the hand-clapping gesture (*kashiwade*) of two bows, two claps, then a final bow, which supposedly distinguishes the act of Shinto worship from Buddhist practices. One then takes a single step back, bows ever so slightly to inform the deity that one's business is completed, and walks back down the steps, turning before departing to enact a last bow of farewell and gratitude.

The final station on the "correct" course includes a

stop at the shrine's information and amulet counter, the *juyosho* ("place of bestowing blessings"), to purchase a talisman (¥800), amulet (¥500–800), set of postcards (¥600), telephone calling card (¥500–2,000) [¥ refers to Japanese yen; ¥100 equals around one dollar], or some other item to remind one of the shrine and one's visit there and to incur the protection of the deity. Legally speaking, the shrine does not "sell" these objects lest it endanger its tax-exempt status; a visitor makes a "donation" and receives these objects in return.

Shrine Visitors Are on Their Own

After all is said and done, it is hard to imagine why anyone should follow or even be able to follow the priests' course of visitation and worship. At Kamigamo Shrine, like the majority of shrines in Japan, visitors are on their own to do the right thing, since there are neither visual markers nor written instructions about what constitutes a correct course, nor do people have the opportunity (were they so inclined) to talk to priests to find out. With the administrative offices outside the central shrine compound (and for good reason, too, since, as one priest said, "not all that goes on in an office do you want the *kami* to know about"), there is a high likelihood that many visitors will not even see a priest during their visits, not to mention have an opportunity to talk to one. Additionally, were a visitor to peruse all the available literature about the shrine available at the amulet counter, he or she would find nothing on the topic of ritual propriety for visitors.

To doctrinally minded Western clerics or missionaries, this laxity of prescribed practices would seem a breeding ground for all sorts of "heretical" or "illicit"

religious behavior. Yet, contemporary Shinto's tolera-
tion of innovative and highly personal forms of worship, some of which will be explored below, is one of its
most important characteristics.

Whose Visit Is It?

If an archetypal visit can be constructed based on data
from my observations, most individuals coming to
Kamigamo are sightseers first, what one might call "exchange practitioners" second, and frequently but not
always "worshipers" last. . . . The first group participates by a slow amble through the sumptuously cared
for grounds, pausing at various buildings to glance
briefly at the marker indicating the name but rarely lingering to read the entire description. The second group,
although they do not engage in acknowledging the
deities, may nonetheless want some pragmatic interaction with the shrine and so purchase a fortune (*omikuji*)
or amulet (*omamori*) as part of their visit.

But by and large the third group is the largest and
most complex, combining the activities from all three
groups yet more conspicuously exhibiting some form
of outward gesture of genuflection, deference, or ac-
knowledgment that they have come to a place requir-
ing a certain kind of behavior. Whether they do so because some feel the *kami* is present, because their sense
of ritual propriety requires it, or because it is simply an
acceptable social form of interaction with the place, I
am still reluctant to assert that observations of and con-
versations with these individuals reflect their true religious beliefs or that social practices are functionally
equivalent with inner dispositions. Once inside Kamigamo's inner courtyard, visitors labor up the rather steep

stone steps until reaching the Middle Gate, through which only priests, ritual participants, and authorized individuals may pass. Before this final barrier, on a gray limestone platform some three by six meters, a wide variety of actions and styles of what appears to be worshipful behavior can be observed. The principal activity signifying what religious scholar Catherine Bell calls "interaction [with the deity] from the bottom up"—and which most Westerners would recognize as the only private moment an individual has at a shrine—is the *kashiwade* (more formally, *hairei*). About half the time, visitors make a small monetary donation into a large wooden coffer-box, then, after bowing twice, raise their hands to chest level and clap twice more. In standardized practice, taught at the training universities for priests, performing *kashiwade* is straightforward and simple, taking no more than fifteen seconds. However, the manifestations and transmutations of this basic gesture are many and varied, some of which are multiple hand claps interspersed by moments of prayer, multiple bows of varying angles (it would appear that the deeper the bow, the more intense the petition), a prolonged prayer (much as one might do in front of a Buddhist altar), and claps arranged into a rhythmic sequence.

No Normative Pattern

Once again, there is no normative pattern of worship prescribed by the shrine and promoted as such. The priests have been educated in upholding the propriety of certain ritual gestures, but, as specialists, they do not impose these traditions on the visitors. While the majority of people simply toss a coin, clap their hands a couple times while bowing, then move on to the next site, there are other regular performances at the Middle Gate. Described below are three frequent visitors to the shrine who illustrated some of the possibilities for what may constitute a shrine visit in contemporary Japanese society. Their dramatic and apparently sincere behavior, rather than being considered aberrations, should be located along a continuum of ritual practices that find common motivation in conveying to spiritual entities a highly personal agenda:

Three Typical Shrine Visitors

Mr. N., from a suburb of southern Kyoto, comes regularly in the morning on the fifteenth of every month to petition the *kami*. A rather tall man of sturdy proportions, twenty-five to thirty years of age, he is always immaculately dressed in a double-breasted suit, with slicked-back hair and shoes shined to a sparkle. Bypassing the font for cleansing one's hands and mouth, his first station is the middle of the Tower Gate entrance, where he plants his feet wide apart and enacts the *kashiwade* with sweeping gestures that indicate an affection for sumo wrestling. Then, he ascends the stairs and finds two stones in front of the Middle Gate, positioning his feet in a manner not unlike a baseball player stepping up to the plate to bat. Legs wide apart, he flexes his knees, rolls his shoulders, and clears his throat before fixing his gaze in the direction of the inner sanctuary. Pulling a folded piece of paper from a suit pocket, he opens the first of many folds and begins his own invocational prayer, modeled on the *norito* prayer format given by a Shinto chief priest while seated before the altar. At first the words are slow and distinct: "O great *kami*, hear the petition of N., from X, who addresses you in awe and gratitude." However, soon after the prologue, the speed doubles, then triples, until Mr. N. is ripping along like a Buddhist priest during a rite to say the *nenbutsu* [the Buddha Amida's name] a million times. Even with this speed, his petition usually takes ten minutes to deliver. The attendant of the upper amulet counter adjacent to the Middle Gate says that Mr. N. is always on time, always stands in the same place, and always leaves without acknowledging anyone. His monetary offering to the shrine is discreetly slipped into the wooden coffer at the beginning of his petitioning and never placed in an envelope that might give away the identity of its donor.

Mr. H., a man in his late fifties, makes the trip from Yokohama to Kyoto once a month between the first and the fifth (the bullet train both ways costs around 23,000 yen or, as of this writing, around U.S. $210) to pay respects to the power of Wake Ikazuchi. Unlike Mr. N., he is quite open about his motives for making this journey:

> I believe this *kami* to be great and fearful, largely because I was granted a vision at Kōyama [the shrine's sacred mountain] shortly before the terrible typhoon of 1991. It was a beautiful day in early August, still and hot, but not sticky like it usually is, and I had gone to the mountain as is my custom. Suddenly, even though there was no wind, the thick growth of trees and vegetation on the southern face of the mountain became agitated, as if moved by a great wind. However, there was no wind at that moment— so how did it happen? The very next day, typhoon nineteen hit Japan—eventually extending from Kyushu to northern Honshu—causing damage like we haven't had from a single typhoon in years. The *kami* of thunder and lightning gave me a message, and I've been trying to ready myself for the next one ever since. I do *misogi* [purification by flowing water]

daily and have formed a group of people in Yokohama to talk, study, and experience this austerity so that we might be closer to the spiritual world.

He performs the *kashiwade* not once but three times in succession. On completion of his worship, Mr. H. always makes it a point to visit the priests at the administration building and keep them up-to-date on his group's activities.

Mrs. S., age seventy-plus from Ōtsu city, struggles up the steps to the Middle Gate twice a month, then sits on the stone *seiza* style (with legs tucked under the buttocks as the knees and shins support and carry one's body weight). There, hands held together in the Buddhist-style *gasshō*, she mutters a prayer of some five minutes while gently swaying back and forth. I am told that she is not the only woman who sometimes kneels on the stone, but for a man to do it would be "very unusual" or, in the words of another priest, "out of the question." One day, on her way back to the bridge over the river, she picked up little red berries on the path beside the Mitarashi stream, bowed to the hillside the berry bush grows on, then found a suitable spot to kneel beside the gently flowing water. She cradled the berries in one hand and, beginning what seemed to be a prayer, methodically tossed them one by one into the stream. Despite the soft morning rain, she did not wear a jacket or carry an umbrella. When the berries were all gone, she bowed to the stream, walked across the bridge to the second torii [gate], turned and bowed once again in the direction of the inner sanctuary, and slowly ambled away.

From the above accounts, it is clear that despite the exalted rank of Kamigamo's principal *kami*, Wake Ikazuchi, and the fact that there is no physical representation of him offered to the public eye, many people supply their own religious framework and establish what may loosely be termed a patron-client relationship with the deity. Requests cover an entire range of human problems and hopes, and are most conspicuously on view at the racks where one hangs an inscribed wooden placard, the *ema*.

[Shinto scholar] Ian Reader has called *ema* "letters to the gods" that "offer a channel whereby Japanese people may therapeutically liberate their feelings in an individual way that enables them to transcend the restrictions of their social milieu". He has given a full analysis of the practice of buying and presenting *ema* plaques. I might only add that if one surveys even a few of the petitionary messages written on the reverse of these colorful placards, it becomes clear that "turning to the gods in times of trouble" (*kurushii toki no kami-danomi*) extends from toothaches, to wayward husbands or uninterested girlfriends, to an upcoming entrance examination. *Ema* provide another means whereby an individual can participate with and become a part of a shrine in a physical way. To externalize one's hopes, desires, troubles, and anxieties on a piece of wood and then leave it in the company of hundreds of other such placards is to join a community of petitioners. Often, an individual reads a number of *ema* before placing his or her own, as if surveying the neighborhood where one's request will best fit in. And while one cannot know for certain what degree of belief accompanies such actions, as they occur within a religious context, are often accompanied by bows, and specifically address the *kami*, I would agree with Reader that they serve as reminders, commitments, and insurance factors in an uncertain world.

Modern Women Enjoy Some Freedoms as Shrine Officials

by John K. Nelson

Women have always held important, if clearly delineated, roles in Shinto worship. Most commonly, young women have served as shrine attendants who perform ritual dances during worship ceremonies. Some translations of early Shinto documents refer to these attendants, known in Japanese as *miko*, as "sacred maidens" or even "shrine virgins," since they were supposed to be unmarried. More rarely, women have served as full-fledged priestesses. As John K. Nelson, the author of the following selection, indicates, the only period when women were not welcome in positions of authority in Shinto shrines was during the nationalistic Meiji era (1868–1912).

In recent times Shinto priestesses have again emerged. Most of the following selection consists of an interview with one such priestess, working at Suwa shrine in Nagasaki. Although the priestess, a Ms. Mine (pronounced "me-nay"), comes from a family of priests and priestesses and takes her religious duties very seriously, she still considers herself a fully modern Japanese woman who played in a rock band while in college and looks forward to shopping sprees and eating in nice restau-

John K. Nelson, *A Year in the Life of a Shinto Shrine*. Seattle: University of Washington Press, 1996. Copyright © 1996 by the University of Washington Press. All rights reserved. Reproduced by permission.

rants. She complains that within the shrine, and despite her certification as a full priestess, she is often given less responsibility than the male priests.

_____

Women had considerable influence in the shrines as spirit mediums or performers of sacred dances [since the rise of organized Shinto], and some shrines had full-fledged priestesses down to the end of the sixteenth century. There were also spirit mediums not directly employed by shrines who served as consultants to both the priests and the parishioners and who operated on or near shrine precincts all through the Edo period [1600–1868]. All this decisively ended with the advent of the Meiji Reformation of 1868, when an edict intended to separate Shinto from Buddhism (so the former could be better manipulated as a rallying point for expansionist goals) also turned out many women who had been until that time legally employed at shrines and denied them the option of recertification.

The beginning of this period of refocusing the symbols and ideas of Shinto was especially restrictive regarding women. But as many smaller, local shrines were deprived of their priests when the militarists called more and more men to serve in the armed forces, an opportunity again arose for women. Since someone had to serve the local Kami [deities], the parishioners, more often than not, pressed the head priest's wife into fulfilling the necessary obligations instead of someone from another region not familiar with the particulars of the community. Presumably, the earlier edict prohibiting women from being priests was pragmatically amended during the war years, because many women did gain the necessary education and certification required to serve as heads of shrines.

Few Restrictions for Female Devotees

Shinto priests have always been free to marry and raise families, so, similarly, nothing prevents priestesses from choosing a spouse and having children. Unlike the monastic tendencies of Buddhism and some schools of Daoism [or Taoism], where to find personal enlightenment or salvation a devotee frequently must leave his family, renounce his social obligations, and endure an indefinite period of asceticism, Shinto is quite accepting of the human condition. After all, it is a natural urge of human beings to seek affection and then honor it by making a commitment to another person, thus gaining recognition as a full-fledged member of society. In many ways this attitude (like many others) was strongly influenced by Confucian ideals, but it has remained a central part of the underlying "social" bond linking a community to their Kami.

About the only prohibition still in effect for women today comes not from a governmentally regulated source but from one of the earliest myths expressed in the *Kojiki* [ancient Japanese chronicles]. It indirectly implies that because blood is thought to be a defiling impurity in the eyes of the Kami, menstruating women should not take part in ritual activities. Once the temporary state of impurity has passed and a priestess has been ritually purified just like any other priest, she can then resume her duties. It should be mentioned that all of this is merely an ideal requirement; whether priestesses or *miko* are actually this strict today about "following the rules" is rather unlikely.

By far the most common role that women play at a contemporary shrine is that of the *miko*—a word that can be cross-culturally referenced (but not translated) as "unmarried female shrine attendant." In a tradition that goes back to the very heart of shamanic practices in Japan—where spirit possession by the Kami was an integral part of the services performed by *miko*—they are today relegated to a variety of important, yet subordinate, roles in relation to the predominantly male priests. In their white kimonos and striking vermilion bloomers, these young women, usually just out of high school, perform a variety of tasks at the shrine during their tenure. In many shrines, their most important role is to perform the sacred *kagura* dance (called *otome-mai*) during all kinds of festivals and rituals. However, not all shrines have *otome-mai* as part of the worship service, in which case the *miko* are still *miko* but they will be found serving as secretaries in shrine offices, as waitresses when guests are treated to a meal in the *naorai* feast (coming immediately after a service), as musicians, messengers, or clerks at an information desk that provides details on how to arrange a private service or on which amulets are appropriate for which situation. The young women are usually recommended by some parishioner or recruited from local families of good repute and hence they generally do not live at the shrine. Though they receive a very modest salary, they are compensated in other ways by the respect they receive from parishioners as well as by the opportunities they have to learn proper etiquette, calligraphy, painting, cooking, and organizational skills—accomplishments that contribute to their eligibility as office employees or as potential wives when they eventually decide to get married.

In talking to Ms. Mine, one of the first things she

points out is that she is most definitely *not* a *miko*. While not demeaning the role of these young women, her insistence on this point will be obvious from the following comments.

A Shinto Priestess Speaks

"I like the feeling of being able to walk down the street, looking just like any other woman my age, and to have this little secret that I'm a Shinto priestess. I guess everyone in Japan wants to have something that makes him or her unique—whether it's fashion, a hobby, or some special ability. I'm proud to be who I am, even though it is a bit unusual for a woman in this day and age.

"My family is a Shinto family and has been in charge of the village shrine at Aino for longer than anyone can remember. When I was in high school, I promised my grandfather to study Shinto when I got older, thinking at the time that it would be a good way to get to Tokyo from my little village down in Kyushu. I was like anyone else who watched TV and had their favorite singers and shows; I thought that Tokyo was where it was all happening, and to have the excuse to study at Kokugakuin University was just perfect. Strangely enough, my parents supported me all the way.

"But maybe I should say a Little about my high school days first. I was very typical, commuting to Isahaya from Aino every day (about ten miles) so I could have the advantages of a larger school. The only time I felt a little different was when I'd have to take special holidays so I could return home to help with a festival or important ritual which my grandfather was in charge of. Then all my friends would tease me, 'Oh, poor Mine; the unfortunate child of a shrine!' However, I thought nothing of it, because there were students there from temple families, merchants' families, or who lived above their fathers' medical clinics who also had to help out from time to time—so it seemed normal. By the way, I should say that my father is a teacher and the only son of my grandfather. It's rather complicated why he didn't go into the shrine but it has something to do with the feeling people had for Shinto after the war. Since many people had grown up with the government forcing Shinto down their throats and since it was used as the justification for imperialism, it wasn't very popular following Japan's defeat. But that's another story however.

"The only time I really felt different from everyone else was when we finally went our separate ways after the senior year—some to nursing school, some to educational teacher-training junior colleges, others to become office girls in various companies in the area, and of course some to get married. But I went away to a university specializing in Shinto studies to become a priestess! That's when everyone started saying, 'What a strange thing you are!' It bothered me a little but when I got to Tokyo, all that was quickly forgotten.

"I know there's a stereotype of Kokugakuin University as being the place where the fanatics who caused so much trouble and got us into World War II went to be indoctrinated, and I was expecting to find something like this. However, it was pretty much a typical university, save that its specialty was Shinto studies, and I led a typical college student's life. I even played keyboards in a rock band—does that surprise you? To be honest, I was probably more interested in music, especially what was happening on the West Coast of America, than I was in learning about Shinto ethics or mythology, but eventually I matured and got serious about my studies.

"At one point during my university days, we had to undergo a training period. You know, the kind that is supposed to make you tough and pure and bright. We had to get up at 4:30 in the morning and thoroughly clean the shrine and gardens surrounding it, then study hard all day, even doing some meditation, and weren't allowed to sleep until 11:00 at night. The worst part was having to perform the *misogi* purification in the ocean while reciting the Oharae prayer about all the impurities and evils that we were washing away. Miyagi Prefecture is north of Tokyo, so that when we did it first in winter I was absolutely frozen to the bone. I remember thinking, 'Ah, so this is what they really mean!' There were only a few other women in my class but we all participated alongside the men. Other than that intense training session, it was all pretty much routine study.

"When I got out of school, I kept my promise to my grandfather and returned to Aino, and through his connections to Suwa Shrine, it was agreed that I come and further my studies. Now that I'm out in society, meeting a variety of people all the time, when they ask me what I do and I answer that I'm a priestess, their reaction is usually the same. 'Incredible!' they say. But this is my career and it seems very normal to me. I'm sure I'll have a relationship with a shrine all my life, even after marriage. If you ask what my career goals are I'd have to say that they're not easy to pinpoint in the way other young people talk about becoming the head of the department or making lots of money or marrying some up-and-coming young executive or doctor. No, for me, what I'd like to do is to make whatever shrine I'm involved with a place where people can come and feel like they are 'home' and want to linger.

"Maybe it's because I'm from a rural area where the

shrine is old and there is a feeling of intimacy between the community members and the shrine, but I don't get that feeling from Suwa Shrine. Actually, I liked the old shrine buildings better before all the remodeling and rebuilding took place. Of course, it is really a splendid-looking place now and is growing and financially sound, yet I can't help feeling that people aren't as close to it as they used to be. Maybe because the Gūji [high priest] spent so much time in Tokyo and his all-business manner gets things done so efficiently, and that his way of doing things is not a Nagasaki way, which is slower and probably more haphazard, but I do feel there is too much emphasis on nonspiritual matters. People need to be able to come to the shrine and feel, 'Ah, I'm glad I came,' and I don't know whether this feeling is as strong as it used to be. But on the other hand, I know very well that if the Gūji doesn't do what he's doing, I won't be able to have money to eat!

"I guess the biggest problem I face now is the old attitudes about women and what their role is supposed to be at a modern shrine such as this one. I don't have hard training or anything like that, other than the juvenile tasks I'm expected to perform because of my rank, which I suppose are similar to pouring tea or making copies in an office. It just seems that other priests, the men, who are licensed the same as me and of my rank do much more than I do. Maybe it's because people might be put off when they come to the shrine and see a woman officiating. They might say, 'Hey, there are men priests here—what's a woman doing at the ritual I'm paying for?' This is discrimination of course, and in a place like Nagasaki, which is still conservative and old-fashioned and where men are believed to be superior to women, I can't escape it, even here at the shrine.

A Shinto priestess prepares fish for a ritual.

"But you know, women have always had an important role in Shinto, right from the very beginning, whenever that was. The first priests were not men but women. Have you heard of Himiko? She was very powerful, not only as a priestess but also as one of the first rulers of Japan. Even today, at Ise Shrine [Shinto's chief shrine], there is a woman priestess higher in rank than the chief priest. The problem is that most people outside the shrine don't know these facts, and that people within the shrine tend to be patriarchal because of their age and education.

"When I first came here I was participating in some of the rituals as a musician and attendant who places mats and helps with whatever the senior priests don't do, but recently I spend most of my time in the information office, selling amulets and writing requests for personalized rites. I'm not a *miko*, you know! But I can't do anything about it because the senior priest in charge of deciding who participates in what ritual is an older man. When it's a simple monthly service like that given for the women's club, well, maybe then I'll be allowed to play flute or the *shō*, but when a more important occasion comes along, I feel like I'm something outsiders shouldn't see. Car purifications, infant dedications, and maybe an occasional wedding, yes, but I really would like to participate more.

"So I've decided that since this is a big shrine and there are many priests, maybe I should just study other things until I return to my own shrine and learn about festivals from my grandfather. Which is something I'll have to do anyway: learn the way it is done at Aino and not the Suwa Shrine way, even though this is 'big-time' Shinto. Now, I can learn about the various amulets and answer questions concerning them and shrine activities, plus learn how to use a word processor and keep things organized in the business office—so I'm doing my best. But, to speak frankly, always being here at the information desk gets a little monotonous. I'd like to bring my Walkman and sit here listening to music but I'm afraid that wouldn't look too good.

"If I could change something about Shinto—whether it's the shrine at Aino or Nagasaki or wherever—I'd like to somehow restore the presence of the Kami to a more direct feeling or contact. It seems that people feel the Kami is something far away, that they have to go to a shrine or be at the family altar before they can share things with the deities. But for me, I think it's a fundamental part of Shinto to have a sense that the Kami is with you, so that if something happens or you need guidance, you can communicate with it immediately, wherever you are. This closeness to the Kami is something our modern civilization and society have completely lost.

"Though this might sound contradictory to you, I see myself as a thoroughly modern Japanese woman and not as some traditionalist. I mean, I like to go on shopping sprees, eat delicious food in fashionable restaurants, hope to get a driving license, or date the person I choose just like anyone else. That's normal, right? When I talk by phone to my friends who are still in Tokyo, I feel like I want to leave the next day and go to a place that will give me more freedom. But the feeling passes; I think because I know deep down that this place I'm in now is where I really belong. Eventually I'll go back to Aino and assume my place in the community after my grandfather retires, but it's still exciting to me to be here in Nagasaki, walking down the street just like anyone else, and to wear my mask which hides my role as a priestess. No one can guess!"

One of Shinto's Most Popular *Kami*, Inari, Is Worshipped in Diverse Ways and Forms

by Karen A. Smyers

Shinto followers believe that the natural world is animated by a divine spirit. The specific manifestations of this divine spirit are known as *kami*, a word which is usually translated as "god" or "spirit" but which might also refer to a natural force or even to a dead ruler who has been deified, such as the Meiji emperor (ruled 1868–1912). The number of *kami* is virtually limitless, but over the course of Japanese history some *kami* have achieved great fame and popularity. Among them are Amaterasu, the sun goddess, and Toyouke, the harvest deity, who are worshipped at Ise (pronounced "eesay"), Shinto's greatest shrine. Another popular *kami*, as the following selection makes clear, is Inari.

Inari, as the author of the selection, Karen Smyers, notes, is associated with the fox by many believers, and this wily creature features frequently in Japanese mythology. In their Inari worship, which takes place in many forms and in many locations, ranging from large urban shrines to small roadside ones, believers commonly ask Inari for various personal blessings. As Smyers writes, however, there is no specific agreement on who or what Inari actually is or represents, and the deity is worshipped by Buddhists as well as Shintoists. Karen Smyers is professor of religion at Wesleyan University.

The deity called Inari has been worshiped in Japan since at least the early eighth century, and today more than one-third of all Shinto shrines in Japan are dedicated to this *kami*. Small Inari shrines without full-time resident priest, home and company shrines, tiny field and roadside shrines are everywhere. If these places were included, the registered number of Inari shrines would increase by ten to one hundred times the official figure. Inari worship is found throughout Japan in both rural and urban settings, and devotees include people from all social classes. Sacred Inari sites may be either Shinto or Buddhist, although the former are more numerous.

Settings of Inari Worship

Sites of Inari worship can be found almost everywhere—in famous large shrines and temples, on factory rooftops, in lay religious establishments, in alleys of major cities, on sacred mountains, in rice fields. Here we consider three representative examples of Inari worship.

Morning Worship at a Tokyo Beauty Salon

The eight staff members of an upscale beauty salon in Roppongi [a Tokyo district] arrive at work by 9:00 and are busily sweeping, dusting, and polishing every surface inside and outside the shop. The space is rather small, but well designed, decorated in elegant high-tech style. The workers are all young and very fashionably attired. When the owner arrives at 10:15, the cleaning stops, and the group lines up behind her under the Inari altar high on the wall just inside the entrance to the shop, complete with fox statues and a tiny offering box. She clasps her hands (glittering with tiny diamonds set into long red fingernails) in prayer, and all follow suit. One of her male assistants stands directly under the altar and formally leads the prayers. They all chant a Shinto *norito* prayer, the Buddhist *Heart Sutra*, then clap and bow twice, and turn and bow to the east, in gratitude to the sun. Private prayers are murmured, and the day begins.

Fall Festival at Toyokawa Inari

Hundreds of red and white paper lanterns decorate the stately precincts of a large Zen Buddhist temple. It is a beautiful fall afternoon, and people of all ages mill around the grounds, listening to the drumming performance of local schoolchildren and eating cotton candy, roasted corn with soy sauce, fried noodles, and other festival favorites. At 3:00, the climax of the festival begins: Inari (here called Dakiniten) is carried from the main sanctuary in a portable shrine *(mikoshi)* to a temporary resting place in front of the shrine of the deity who protects this Buddhist temple.

The procession begins with musicians dressed in ancient court style playing *gagaku* [ceremonial] music on wooden flutes and a drum. Following them are eight priests in splendid brocade robes carrying silver and gold ritual implements, sutras, symbolic keys to the buildings, and a brocade-covered book containing a list of the faithful. As they walk, they purify the grounds and onlookers in three ways: one scatters drops of water from a goblet using a green leaf as a dipper; one carries incense in a receptacle fashioned as a dragon with a magic jewel in its claws; the last scatters flower petals (made of paper). People scramble to retrieve these petals, pushing and shoving anyone in their way. The lucky few who get one consider it to be an extremely efficacious charm and put it carefully into a purse or wallet.

A line of fifty divine children *(chigo)* from age three to seven follows. Escorted by their mothers and wearing gold crowns and bright red, purple, and gold kimonos, they have powdered white faces and red lips like courtiers of old. Some cry in fear, others ham it up for the video cameras. The procession passes under a large stone torii gate and past the gazes of two pairs of large guardian fox statues. Finally comes the Inari deity, borne in a splendid gold palanquin by thirty young men and women in short pants and *happi* coats, sweating and groaning under the staggering weight. They weave drunkenly back and forth across the path, careening into the crowds, tipping and shaking the deity. Behind this, at a safe distance, walks the head priest of the temple, in a bright red robe, shaded by a large umbrella held over his head by an attendant. Two large white foxes prance along, oversize masks borne on the shoulders of two men, and worshipers place money into their open mouths as offerings for luck. The palanquin comes to a rest under a large tree, and the priests conduct a short Buddhist worship service. The head priest prostrates himself on the ground, offers incense, and chants a sutra. After the prayers, the priests slowly walk away, and the informal festival activities resume.

In the evening, the paper lanterns are lit, shining a soft red into the black night.

Crossroads Divination at Hyōtan Yama Inari

The shrine known as Hyōtan Yama Inari is located in the outskirts of Osaka in the foothills. Its name derives from the shape of the hill on which it sits, which resembles a guitar-shaped gourd *(hyōtan)* lying on its side. This auspiciously shaped mountain was also used as a burial chamber *(kofun)* sometime between the third and sixth centuries. Now the shape of the hill is obscured by the tall buildings that cluster around it, but this shrine is still well known for crossroads divination. I visited it on March 4, 1990, with the head priest from another Inari shrine and his two young sons. The shrine grounds were impressive: although small, they contained a profusion of fox statues, *otsuka* worship stones, and various forms of popular devotion. Here the wish-fulfilling jewel usually found at Inari worship sites is not in evidence but has been replaced by the *hyōtan* gourd, which appears as decorative motif on most surfaces. Wanting to learn about the crossroads divination, we went first to the shrine office and got instructions about how to proceed. The priest there explained with a detailed map exactly what to do. First I made a small monetary offering at the main sanctuary and asked Inari for assistance in answering my question. Then I shook a cylindrical wooden box containing three long rods until one fell out the small hole at the bottom. It was Number 1, which indicated that I should pay attention to the first person who passed and note the manner of passing (walking, running, car, bicycle), dress, sex, items carried, and so on. Next I walked around to the left of the shrine and followed the path to the back gate, which looked out onto a paved road running perpendicular to the path. There was a stone to mark the spot, and there I waited. Soon the buzzing of a mini-motorbike could be heard, and I waited with interest for its arrival. In a moment, a man on a bright red motorbike passed from my left to right and disappeared over the hill and round a curve.

We went back to the shrine office and were seated in a tatami-mat room where we waited on cushions while the head priest concluded his previous audience. I was instructed to put on a white vest, a garment symbolizing my purity for the divination. Finally we were ushered into the priest's old-fashioned room, which held an Inari altar in the alcove consisting of a miniature antique shrine building of dark wood and two very old earthenware white fox statues. The priest asked me the particulars of who had passed, and he filled in the information on a printed worksheet. He then turned and sat facing the Inari altar and prayed. The question I had posed for this divination was whether my study of Inari would be published as a book. The priest said yes: because a *man* had passed from north to south, it meant this task was possible. Men work in the world, so this was a very good sign. Looking at the expression on my face, he hastened to point out that women work very hard too, but in Japan it is usually within the home. The motorbike indicated that the task would not take too long. The other priest thought that the bike's bright red color reinforced the meaning of Inari as subject of the book, because red is the distinctive color that identifies Inari shrine buildings. The head priest then told us in great detail of his fascination with the theory that the Japanese are actually one of the lost tribes of Israel.

After discussing this question, we thanked the priest, took some photographs, and paid the 2,000-yen fee for the divination.

In Search of Consensus

Inari worship may be conducted by Shinto or Buddhist priests, by nonclerical religious specialists, by lay worship group leaders, or by devotees themselves. Festivals involving the whole town or large numbers from an urban area celebrate Inari's blessings collectively, and priests conduct dozens of prayer services (gokittō) daily for individuals or small groups. Devotees ascertain the divine will in various "folk" methods of divination that do not require a priest or religious specialist and may even experience Inari personally through a possession or divine dream. I use the term "religious specialist" to differentiate the healers and shamans from the priests, both Shinto and Buddhist. In Japanese, these religious specialists are called odaisan, ogamiyasan, reinōsha, or reikanshi. They often head lay worship groups (kō), but to classify them with ordinary lay leaders slights the tremendous religious power they command. Followers often consider them to be far more religiously advanced than the priests, who they describe as "learning about religion from books, not by doing austerities.". . .

Many Japanese not involved personally with Inari told me they assumed that all Inari worshipers are elderly or interested only in financial gain. Older people and those praying for business prosperity (shōbai hanjō) are indeed numerous, but I also met worshipers from a fairly representative cross section of Japan: fashionable young hairdressers, an elite company president and his staff, housewives, families and children, a silk weaver, a truck driver, a medical doctor and his patients, musicians, gangsters, a photographer, spiritualists, a real estate agent, liquor store owners, an orange farmer, an alcoholic, students, very ill people, shopkeepers, a baker, flower arrangement and tea ceremony instructors, brewers, train workers, insurance workers, an oil company head, a doctor's wife, a chiropractor, geisha, sushi bar owners, and local politicians.

No matter where the worship of Inari takes place or who conducts it, one or more symbols most likely will be present: the fox, jewel, red torii, red worship hall, prayer flags, rock altar, cedar, fried tofu, and rice. Because of these symbols, Inari shrines are easy to distinguish—unlike so many other shrines where even the locals can only answer a generic *"kami sama"* (honorable deity) in answer to the question of what deity is enshrined there. Inari worship sites can almost always be identified by their red color and prominent pair of fox statues. But is Inari always the same deity? Are Shinto priests, Buddhist priests, and shamanic religious specialists worshiping the same Inari? Are there doctrinal differences between the different institutional centers?

Although settings of worship are diverse, they symbolize Inari in a fairly consistent way through the use of an easily recognizable set of symbols. But when people speak about Inari, this seeming unity quickly dissolves into a bewildering array of understandings—many of which are completely contradictory. It might be reasonably thought that this is probably the situation in most religions. Perhaps one should consult the experts, those who take as normative certain doctrinal or historical materials. To some extent, I attempted to do this. But I quickly learned there was little consensus among priests or scholars either.

Ideas About Inari

The most often heard ideas about Inari are that it is a Shinto *kami* that is (or is connected with) a fox. But when I asked Shinto priests about the identity of Inari, they had various ideas. Some identified Inari with Uganomitama no Ōkami, a *kami* from the classical mythologies; others linked Inari with Toyouke no Kami, the *kami* worshiped in the outer shrine at Ise; still others took Inari to be equivalent to any grain *kami*. The pamphlets distributed by Inari shrines throughout Japan include a bewildering array of *kami* enshrined as Inari. The one thing most priestly commentators agreed upon is that Inari has a deep connection to rice.

A bit more investigation, especially among scholars and priests, reveals that Inari is worshiped in Buddhist temples as well—often as the temple protector *(chin-jugami)* but sometimes as the main object of worship. At Toyokawa Inari, the setting of the fall festival described earlier, the Buddhist form of Inari is called Dakiniten. At Saijō Inari in Okayama, a Nichiren [Buddhist] sect temple, the main object of worship is the *Lotus Sutra*, but here it takes the form of a deity called Saijō-sama. Both Buddhist Inaris take the form of a bodhisattva carrying rice astride a flying white fox.

Worshipers at these various sacred sites had rather diverse ideas about Inari. Some were simply vague, such as the man whose family had worshiped for years what they assumed was Inari in their home shrine—only to open the doors and discover an entirely different *kami* enshrined there. Many were completely unaware of Inari's Buddhist form, and one man got very angry with me when I insisted that Toyokawa Inari was a Buddhist temple. Another was open-mindedly eclectic: "Inari is really a [Shinto] *kami* but is worshiped at Toyokawa as a

Buddhist deity—but I really feel it is more of a *kami* than a Buddhist figure. I don't think Inari is different from other *kami*, and may even be the same as the Christian God. The point for me is that *kami* have a lot of power—the particular variety of that strength is not important." Others had more personalized views. One woman who worshiped both the *kami* of the new religion of Tenrikyō as well as Inari "discovered" Inari to be one of the ten deities of that religion. Another devotee, the fervent leader of an Inari lay worship group under the auspices of the Fushimi Inari Shrine, realized one day that Inari had been responsible for the economic recovery of the Volkswagen company. He had heard about the decline and recovery of the company, and when he saw that the logo of the company was a fox, realized that "Inari's powers work even in foreign countries."

When Inari is visualized by devotees or depicted in iconography, gender is variable (and so I use both masculine and feminine pronouns to refer to Inari). Unlike other well-known Japanese deities who have unambiguous gender in anthropomorphic form, Inari is thought to be either male or female; or both; or neither. Its most popular representations are as an old man carrying rice, a young female food goddess, or an androgynous bodhisattva on a white fox. Priests and devotees offer justifications for their understanding of the gender of this deity, but there is no theological orthodoxy on this question. The deity Inari was worshiped on the sacred mountain in Fushimi from at least the eighth century, and it was not until some centuries later that priests tried to identify this deity with others from the official mythology. Inari seems not to have been gendered at first: the female associations come from Inari's functions as a rice and fertility deity; the male associations derive from later Buddhist traditions.

The one constant I did discover in priestly rhetoric about Inari, Shinto and Buddhist alike, was that it discourages the idea that Inari is a fox. Nevertheless, many people believe this to be the case. Some saw Inari to be a benevolent fox-*kami;* others were frightened of it. One said, "Dakiniten is a fox-*kami* who eats people and is terrifying." A souvenir shop near the grounds of the Fushimi Inari Shrine considered a statue of a fox to be the repository *(shintai)* of Inari and would not let me photograph it. The priests were appalled by the notion when I described it to them. Another idea I encountered almost as often as the fox identification was the notion that Inari is a snake (or dragon)—but this does not seem to upset the priests to the same extent that the fox does. From time to time I was told that Inari is incarnate in the body of a living devotee, usually a shamanic female who can speak for the *kami.*

A Personal Deity

Inari is both loved and feared. People involved with this deity tend to feel great intimacy with her; those less involved may be nervous about the stories of her retribution related with great relish even in modern-day Tokyo. In either case, people consider Inari to be a very powerful deity: the "rough" or "wild" side is not necessarily evil; it is simply the deity's inherent power to reward or punish. I was told by a very cosmopolitan Tokyo boutique owner about the recent removal of a tiny Inari shrine to build a skyscraper. An unusual number of accidents and injuries began to make the workers very nervous—but after they replaced the Inari shrine, the accidents stopped. Priests too respect the

A fox statue sits before a Kyoto shrine dedicated to Inari.

notion that Inari's anger is to be taken seriously. An Inari shrine in Kyushu was established in 829 on the basis of a divine dream to avert a plague. The traditional date to celebrate the festival to this Inari is September 20, but some years ago the priests moved the main part of the festival to the nearest Sunday so that more people could attend. In the late 1980s, one of the large floats fell over and killed three people during the festival. The head priest and two others made a pilgrimage of propitiation to the Fushimi Inari Shrine, fearing that Inari was angry because of the date change. Moreover, they tried to appease Inari by inviting priestesses *(miko)* from the Fushimi shrine to perform their sacred *kagura* dance at the Kyushu shrine as an offering.

For the majority of worshipers with whom I talked, however, Inari's other side was more important. People constantly told me of their personal connections to Inari, their profound intimacy with this *kami*, and their deep gratitude to Inari for countless blessings received. Still, even this special relationship gave them no license to slight Inari, and their intimacy did not include careless behavior toward this deity. It is important to note that people who may be very involved in Inari worship (as well as other religious practices) may not consider themselves particularly religious. This is partly a problem of semantics, for the term "religion" *(shūkyō)* implies adherence to specific religious groups and doctrines. But it also shows the contradictory positions a person may hold. A female lay worker at the Toyokawa Inari Temple provides a good example of this in her own "half belief/half doubt" along with great respect for the religious experiences of others:

> Well, I sort of half believe and half don't *(hanshin-hangi).* I suspect this is the attitude of most of the priests and lay workers at this temple: we are fairly practical about Inari because this is our job and livelihood. This is very different from the real devotees who come here, who are fervent about their faith. I imagine that this faith has a positive effect on their lives. One woman told me an experience she had when she returned to this temple to express her thanks. Her son was very sick, and she came here and prayed and got a talisman *(ofuda)* from this temple. Sitting by her son's sickbed, she dozed off and had a dream in which Dakiniten suddenly loomed up in the sky. When she awoke, her son's fever was gone, but her own chest hurt as if a weight were crushing down upon it. She did not see the talisman, and searched all over for it, finally locating it under a heavy book. When she removed it from under this heavy weight, her own chest stopped hurting.

Shinto Ideas Shape Japanese Culture

by C. Scott Littleton

In the following selection author C. Scott Littleton examines how modern Japanese life is shaped by Shinto ideas and assumptions. He places particular emphasis on the notion of *wa*, or benign harmony. *Wa* requires that human societies formulate rules to maintain order; without rules the only result is chaos. Littleton acknowledges that the idea came originally from China and was later reinforced by such Chinese imports as Confucianism. But he also argues that it can be traced to Japan's ancient past, when individuals had to maintain harmony with both their household and with unseen spirits.

Littleton argues that in the modern era, *wa* is the basis for such Japanese customs as group solidarity and the need to show respect and atone for mistakes. Even the habit of taking off one's shoes before entering a house reflects, he claims, the Shinto emphasis on purification. In such ways Shinto's influence is clear even in the fast-paced, wealthy, high-technology Japan of today. A Japan specialist, C. Scott Littleton is professor of anthropology at Occidental College.

One of the most important ancient ethical codes informing Japanese belief and behavior is the prioritization of group solidarity over individual identity. Although to some extent inherited from Chinese culture, this code is powerfully reinforced by Shinto's long-standing emphasis upon the veneration of ancestral spirits, and family, and clan, solidarity.

Of equal significance is the tradition's concentration upon personal and ritual purity, and reverence for nature—all of which are basic tenets of the faith. Such principles have profoundly influenced Japanese behavior, from prehistoric times onward, and have played important roles in the modern Japanese environmental movement—those people caring for local Shinto shrines have often been at the forefront of efforts to clean up the countryside. It is sometimes claimed that the Japanese rely solely on their Buddhist heritage for ethical guidance. However, this does not stand up to scrutiny. At the core of Shinto theology lies the idea that *wa* ("benign harmony") is inherent in nature and human relationships, and that anything that disrupts this state is bad. This helps to explain the widespread and deeply rooted Japanese belief that the individual is less important than the group, be it family, school, or workplace. Rules governing human behavior are considered necessary for the maintenance of *wa*, without which both society and the natural world would disintegrate into chaos. This ancient Chinese concept has guided both Japanese Shinto and Buddhist behavior for more than fifteen hundred years.

Confucian and Daoist [or Taoist] ideas imported from China also claimed that chaos would follow if social nonconformity was tolerated, but these concepts served principally to reinforce the existing Shinto ethic, which sprang from the clan-based society of prehistoric and ancient Japan. This ethic revolves around two fundamental and intimately related concepts: the need to maintain the *tatemae* ("face") that a person presents to the outside world; and the *ie* ("extended household"), which includes all the ancestral spirits. The idea that Japanese ethics are based on shame rather than guilt has been exaggerated, but it is nonetheless true that conformity is enforced to a large degree by the loss of *tatemae* that an individual—and consequently his or her *ie*, school, employer, or other social group—would suffer as a result of violating part of the social code. Depending on the seriousness of the loss of face, a person may atone by bowing deeply, by a ceremonial act of gift-giving, or by committing suicide. Even today, suicide is often blamed on a person's inability to cope with the shame of, say, failing an examination.

If a whole group is stigmatized, a collective act of atonement is made. For example, when Japan's famous Shinkansen "Bullet Train" is late, every employee from the engineer to the conductor, hostesses, and ticket sellers feels responsible and will apologize profusely to delayed passengers. Once atonement is made, the shame ceases and the burden it imposes is lifted.

The Shinto ethic reached its apogee during the "State Shinto" era (1872–1945), when obedience to the emperor became the noblest form of behavior—up to and including sacrificing one's life for his benefit. It is very much a "this-worldly" phenomenon, with little or no emphasis placed on reward or punishment in the afterlife. However, the state of the soul after death is very much the concern of Japan's Buddhist traditions. From the outset, Mahayana Buddhism [the Buddhist school predominant in China, Japan, Korea, and Vietnam] has

had a well-defined concept of inherent human wickedness, and the Buddhist's ultimate goal is to achieve salvation in the form of *nirvana*, or release from the cycle
of birth, death, and rebirth. This cycle is fueled by the
accumulation of merit and demerit, a concept known as
karma. In the Buddhist view, demerit springs from desire, and the loss of desire is thus the key to salvation. In
Japan, this deep-rooted Buddhist insistence on suppress-
ing personal desire complements the Shinto ethical tradition that demands subordination to the group in such
a way that *wa* is nourished and maintained.

Anything that contributes to *wa* is, by definition,
good; those things—behavior, emotions, desire, and so
on—that disrupt it are perceived as being fundamentally evil. This belief also applies to humankind's relationship with nature and underscores the pervasive
Shinto concern with maintaining a balance between
the human and natural realms. Indeed, those individuals associated with local Shinto shrines have often taken
the lead in campaigns to clean up rivers and lakes.

The Shinto obsession with *wa* is also reflected in a variety of Japanese customs that, at first glance, might not
seem religious, such as removing one's shoes before entering a house and taking a daily bath (known as *ofuro*).
Both customs are, essentially, expressions not only of
purification—the interior of a home is, after all, a "sacred space" compared to the outside world—but also of
the maintenance of a harmonious balance in the world.

Renewal and purification are, then, persistent themes
of Shinto practice and belief. Every shrine has a trough
containing pure water for the ritual ablutions—rinsing of
the hands and mouth—required before one approaches
the image of the *kami*. The worshiper scoops out some
water with a bamboo dipper, pours it over his or her

hands, and lightly rinses the mouth, thereby purifying the body both inside and out, and making it fit to enter the presence of the gods. The human body is thus cleansed and its internal balance is restored through acts of ritual purification such as these, which are known as *oharai.* A similar ritual is undertaken by *miko* girls ("shrine virgins") when they perform a dance known as a *kagura,* which is a celebration of the renewal of life.

Other important purification and renewal practices include the annual replacement of miniature family shrines and the periodic rebuilding of major shrines in order to invest them with life and vigor. All the buildings in Shinto's most sacred and revered shrine complex, Ise—near the coast southeast of Nara in Mie prefecture—have, since the eighth century, been replaced every twenty years by replicas that are exact copies down to the last wooden peg (the most recent rebuilding occurred in 1993). The symbolism here is extremely important: with each rebuilding both the sun goddess, Amaterasu (the divine ancestor of the imperial house), and the harvest goddess, Toyouke, acquire renewed vigor, and this also ensures the continuing vitality of both the imperial line and the rice crop, without either of which it would be impossible for the nation to survive.

At the end of the twenty-year cycle, the new shrine buildings are erected on a site alongside the old ones. For a brief period, the visitor might be forgiven for experiencing a sense of double vision, because the complex and its copy stand side-by-side until the sacred images have been ritually transferred to the new shrine by the distinctively clad Ise priests. Only then are the old structures dismantled and the ground cleared, to be carefully maintained until the rebuilding cycle comes around again.

The dismantled buildings continue to be imbued with the powerful sacred essence of the goddesses and are not destroyed. Instead, pieces are distributed to shrines throughout Japan and incorporated into their walls, thereby spiritually reinvigorating the entire Shinto universe. The new structures are built by carpenters who typically come from families who have participated in this activity for generations. Thus, the Ise shrines are steeped in ancient tradition, but at the same time always appear new and fresh.

Old Customs Mix with New Ways of Life at a Local Shrine

by Ian Reader

In the following selection scholar Ian Reader examines the interconnections between Shinto worship and festivals and the modern lives of ordinary Japanese. His setting is the Katano shrine, a local shrine in an area between the two cities of Osaka and Kyoto. The area has become suburbanized over the last decades and, as Reader implies, provides a good example of how rural, traditional Shinto has become juxtaposed with the faster pace of modern life. On New Year's eve, for example, Shintoists often watch nationally famous television programs before visiting the shrine to take part in traditional purification rituals and other festivities. Ian Reader is lecturer in contemporary Japanese studies at the University of Stirling in the United Kingdom.

There is a great emphasis in Shinto on beginnings, growth, fertility and celebration, and the events that occur in the lives of individuals, households and communities that bring them into a relationship with the *kami* [gods] and the shrine generally revolve around these themes. The ritual of *miyamairi*, in which the baby is taken shortly after birth to the local shrine to receive the blessing and be placed under the protection of the *kami* who is the guardian of the local community and area, integrates the child into the local community and also, because of Shinto's ethnic themes, into the wider community of Japan. Traditionally the household to which the child belonged was affiliated to the shrine: both individual and household were its *ujiko*, parishioners, under the protection of the *kami* and with various obligations to help in its upkeep and to participate in and contribute to the annual (or seasonal) festivals which helped to draw the community together and provide a sense of social bonding. The shrine often served (and still does in some places) as a community centre, the setting for meetings and recreational activities as well as various religious events. In such terms the local shrine stood as a regional and territorial entity, a focus of the community of identity and belonging. It also formed, especially in earlier times when communications were not so highly developed, a link between the village and the wider Japanese world. Local shrines were often branch shrines of nationally known ones, enshrining *kami* of nationwide repute such as Hachiman, Tenjin, Inari or the *kami* venerated at the shrines of Ise: in fact two-thirds of Shinto shrines today enshrine one of these *kami*. The shrine thus, besides symbolising regional community, acted as a conduit uniting the village and its people with the wider social world of the Japanese nation.

Shrines as Community Centers

In many respects Shinto has been, especially at local levels, more of an amorphous tradition of shrines related to local communities' identities and life cycles, and concerned with the maintenance of a continuing and productive relationship with the *kami* than anything else, and it is these themes that will concern us most here.

Although demographic changes have altered the religious landscape in recent years one can still find shrines that perform a centralising role in their local communities: contemporary change does not always sweep away all vestiges of earlier times. In order to illustrate the workings of Shinto in social terms and shed light on the major events that take place at shrines throughout the country I shall here describe one such shrine. Whether one could call it 'typical' is a difficult question: with approximately 80,000 registered shrines in Japan there is probably no such place. However, the events celebrated and the times when people visit it are standard enough to make it as reasonable a microcosm of the overall as is possible. It is a shrine I came to know well not through academic research but because my wife and I lived near it for two years during which time we came to regard it as 'our' local shrine (in a way that we never had with shrines in other places we had lived in Japan), announcing it as such to those who came to stay with us and making it our first port of call during the New Year's celebrations.

The area in which Katano shrine stands is situated halfway between the cities of Kyoto and Osaka, in an old rice-farming area that has, due to its proximity to both cities, become commuter territory, its fields built over as the population has increased dramatically in recent years. The whole area is a juxtaposition of new housing, old farmhouses, rice fields, apartment blocks, bars, *pachinko* [Japanese pinball] parlours, electrical stores and rice merchants, of frantic businessmen and office girls rushing for trains to the city in the morning, of housewives visiting the local market to buy food, and schoolgirls clustering in the music shop for posters and cassettes of the current idols—in short, the rather typical mixture of old and new, and the crowded jumble of buildings, telegraph wires, narrow streets and level-crossings that may be found virtually anywhere in contemporary urban Japan.

The Katano Shrine

The shrine clearly benefited from the remaining local community of farmers and from the influx of new faces, for it managed to support a full-time priest who could call on the services of a number of assistants, especially *miko*, or shrine maidens, at festivals. Although part of the shrine dated to the sixteenth century and was deemed a prefectural cultural asset it was hardly known outside the local region. Nor was it especially large, the whole area of the shrine, surrounded by an old mud and brick wall, being approximately 60 metres long and 50 wide.

While not attracting people from further afield the shrine was certainly an active centre for the local community. I used to go by it every day on my way to and from work and frequently saw people passing through the shrine and paying their respects to the *kami*. On Sundays there were often several babies being taken on the *miyamairi*, clad in a bright baby *kimono* with several lucky amulets attached to it: the priest would chant Shinto prayers while one of the shrine maidens performed a sacred dance and gave a symbolic purificatory blessing to the baby. The reason that Sundays are the most common day for such activities (and indeed for most shrine and temple visiting) is a pragmatic rather than a religious one: it is the only day most people in Japan have off work and hence the most convenient for such things.

Besides the general flow of passers-by, regular worshippers, babies receiving the *kami's* blessing, people coming to pray for safety because it was their unlucky year (*yakudoshi*), and the occasional wedding that might be celebrated there, the shrine had a number of regular yearly events (*nenjū gyōji*) that punctuated the year. In November the shrine, along with most others in Japan, came alive with the *shichigosan* (7–5–3) festival, in which girls of three and seven and boys of five are taken to the shrine to be further placed under the protective blessings of the *kami*. The chief day for this is 15 November (or, more commonly, the Sunday nearest that date) but the blessings are, as at most shrines, dispensed throughout the month. As with *miyamairi* and New Year it is an occasion for dressing up and for overt display: the children are dressed formally, usually in a bright kimono but sometimes in formal Western-style dress. Their parents also dress up for the occasion, usually in Western style. More and more frequently, in line with the growing economic wealth of the country, the parents are liable, both at *shichigosan* and *miyamairi*, to be carrying expensive cameras or, a prominent feature in the last few years, video cameras to capture the event for posterity. It may not be unreasonable to suggest that events such as these provide an interesting barometer of Japan's economic prowess, with the progression from ordinary cameras to video recorders, and the growing numbers who own the latter, manifesting a continuing display of economic power.

Probably the two most active times at the shrine were the *hatsumōde* period in January and the annual shrine festival in mid-October, and at these two periods the shrine and the surrounding area became alive and active. The former is a nationwide and the latter a local festival specific to the shrine, although it has wider connotations for its roots are in the harvest celebrations that are still celebrated at countless other festivals throughout Japan at this time. There are festivals all the year round in Japan, and it is possible to find one occurring somewhere on virtually every day of the year, but certain periods, such as the beginning of the year, the traditional planting season of spring, the hot months of the summer which are eminently suited to relaxed evening festivals, and the period in mid October are definitely peak times for festivals across the country.

Celebrating the New Year

The New Year's festival is both a national holiday, a time for celebration and relaxation, and a religious event with themes of regeneration, purification and renewal as the old year and whatever bad luck it contained are swept aside in a tide of noisy enjoyment. It is traditional to clean one's house thoroughly and to pay off all debts before the end of the year (indeed I have seen, in the national newspapers, reminders during the last days of the old year that this is the time to clean one's house), thus clearing away physically and metaphorically the residue of the past year so as to allow one to start again new. Throughout January there are numerous 'first' festivals, such as the *hatsu Ebisu* ('first Ebisu') widely celebrated especially in the Kyoto–Osaka region from 9–11 January, which is the first festive day of the year of the popular deity Ebisu. All such festivals reiterate the theme of transition from old to new, of the sweeping away of the hindrances of the past and of fresh beginnings, expressing optimistic hopes for good fortune.

The New Year's festival is the largest of all these, and at this time it is customary to visit shrines (and some of the better-known temples as well) to pay one's respects to the *kami*, to ask for good luck and help in the coming year and to make resolutions fortified by the general mood of optimistic renewal. This is accompanied by a great changeover in religious amulets and talismans as new ones representing the power and benevolence of the *kami* and Buddhas are acquired and old ones are dispensed with. The most commonly procured of these at New Year is the *hamaya* (literally 'evil-destroying arrow'), a symbolic arrow that is placed in the home as a protective talisman to drive away or absorb bad luck. Other lucky charms, talismans and amulets . . . are also on sale at the shrines and temples, the income this produces often making an important contribution to the upkeep of the institutions. Often the talismans that are purchased are placed in the household *kamidana* [altar] thereby creating a further link between shrine and household, with the *kamidana* itself operating as a localised shrine in its own right sacralising the house itself.

At the same time the old amulets and talismans from the previous year are jettisoned, and most shrines and temples at this time designate a special place where these can be left. Some time later, usually in mid-January, these will be formally burnt in a purificatory rite, generally to the accompaniment of priests chanting prayers whose powers, along with the exorcistic nature of the fire, transform the impurities and eradicate the bad luck that have been absorbed by the amulets and talismans. The pollutions and hindrances of the past are thus dispensed with and the way is opened up, symbolised by the acquisition of new charms, for regeneration. Naturally, too, in the process of cyclical transition, those same new talismans will be brought back the next year to be burnt, in a continuing round of change and renewal.

On the evening of 31 December it is customary for families to eat a special seasonal feast together: it has also become something of a custom to watch the television, where a number of musical spectaculars, particularly the *Kōhaku*, a song contest between teams of leading female and male stars that is broadcast by NHK, have become integrated parts of the New Year's Eve ritual. The *Kōhaku* programme ends a little before midnight, giving people enough time to get to their local shrine before the bells chime in the coming year. In both years that I went to Katano shrine a long line of people, most of them in family groups, stood waiting just before midnight in front of a straw ring of purification erected before the shrine. The act of passing through this ring prior to worshipping symbolically removes past pollutions and allows them to greet the *kami* anew. The shrine itself and the houses around it were brightly lit with lanterns, and the crowd numbering around 500 or so bubbled with conversation and anticipation as the priest turned on the radio. This broadcast the sound of the bells of Chionin, a famous Buddhist temple in Kyoto, whose great bell tolls, as do the bells of innumerable Buddhist temples throughout the country, 108 times just before midnight. The number 108 is symbolic for the numerous ills, unhappinesses and evil passions inherent, according to Buddhism, in the world, and the tolling symbolically eradicates them one by one. As the year ends, then, the Buddhist temple plays its part in purifying the past and realigning the world, complementing the shrine through which the coming year is greeted.

Religious Objects

As the tolling ended and the time signal chimed midnight people began to flow through the arch, clapping their hands in prayer, tossing coins into the offertory box and praying. After this they went across to the shrine office where all manner of religious talismans were on sale, including the special *hamaya* of the shrine and wooden votive tablets (*ema*) on which petitions to the *kami* may be written. In the Sino-Japanese system there is a twelve-yearly cycle somewhat akin to the zodiacal system, with each year represented by a different animal, and at this shrine as at many others, the *ema* depicted the year-animal of the coming year. As 1988 was the year of the dragon, the *ema* bore dragon insignia and, in 1989, snakes.

Soon the entire shrine area was crowded, and everyone, or at least every group, appeared to have a *hamaya* and several other talismans besides. Money was spent freely, as is common at festive times when the economic constraints of everyday life are commonly laid aside in favour of the freedoms of the moment. Much of this was at the instigation of children who, in their excitement at staying up so late, were particularly insistent that their parents buy them charms and divination slips. The latter are usually read aloud, with one's friends and family, invariably in a light-hearted manner, and then tied up on the trees or fences in the shrine precincts. The action of tying up the paper strips is done, depending on one's informant, so as to allow the bad luck predicted in the oracle to be blown away by the wind, to share out good luck predicted and thus balance out other people's bad luck or, more prosaically, simply because this is what everyone else does! Whatever explanation may be given, the trees and fences at the shrine, as at any shrine in Japan at New Year, were rapidly festooned with strips of white paper.

Inside the main hall of the shrine the priest chanted sacred Shinto prayers to the accompaniment of shrine music played by assistants while shrine maidens wearing the traditional apparel of a red *hakama*, or split skirt, and white blouse performed *kagura*, sacred dances designed to please the *kami* and facilitate the transfer of the *kami*'s benevolence to the people. Other shrine maidens helped run the office, sell talismans and impart purificatory blessings. Not all of these were trained officiants, for the sheer tide of visitors means that virtually every religious institution needs to take on part-time help in order to cope at this time, and one year I found myself in the crowd being blessed by one of my students performing her temporary job as a shrine maiden!

In the shrine various donations were arrayed from the community and local businesses thanking the *kami* for past support and seeking its continuation. Where feasible it seemed that the neighbourhood shops sent offerings connected with their trade, the rice merchants for instance sending sacks of rice, but when this was not possible the most common offerings were food and sake (rice wine). The gifts were not just from the older and more traditional establishments but also from the newer ones: one of the local beauty salons which catered to the fashionable young of the district, for example, sent two bottles of sake. Sake is a popular offering that can be swiftly recycled after it has been placed on the altar and thus sacralised: thereafter partaking of it becomes a pleasant act of communion with the *kami* that helps one enter further into the spirit of the festival. A stall was set up in the precincts where small cups of shrine sake could be quaffed free: it should be added that no one appeared to indulge in much more than one symbolic cup.

After the first night the shrine became gradually quieter and quieter, returning to normality on 4 January: the *hatsumōde* period really lasts until 3 January at all but the most major shrines. At Katano most people came at or soon after midnight: by 1 A.M. they were moving off elsewhere, either back home or to catch trains to Kyoto or Osaka to visit the larger and more famous shrines and temples there. The trains, which run all night at this period, were packed with revellers either going home clutching *hamaya* or on their way to get them. It was interesting that most of the people in the area made their visit to Katano before going on to the more nationally known centres nearby, a sign perhaps of the continued importance of the shrine to its surrounding community, indicating that local loyalties may still take precedence over wider ones.

A War Memorial Shrine Sparks Controversy

by Bennett Richardson

In the spring of 2005, Chinese protesters staged demonstrations criticizing Japan for denying atrocities committed by Japanese forces during World War II. The inspiration for these protests was a new set of government-approved textbooks, but the controversy is also connected to the subject discussed in the following selection: the Shinto shrine Yasukuni, where Japan's war dead are commemorated. The names of certain Japanese officials executed for war crimes are also included in the memorial. Some Shinto believers hold that those honored at Yasukuni have been turned into gods and should be revered as such, even those condemned as war criminals.

Bennett Richardson, a correspondent for the *Christian Science Monitor*, examines the status of the shrine as well as the disagreements over whether it should remain open as it stands or be replaced by a war memorial with no religious meaning. Bennett also notes how Japanese prime ministers have frequently made ceremonial visits to Yasukuni, angering their Chinese counterparts.

When millions of Japanese gather at shrines across the nation to welcome the New Year [in 2005], all eyes will be focused on where Prime Minister Junichiro Koizumi pays his respects.

Last Jan. 1, Mr. Koizumi went to Yasukuni, a shrine in Tokyo dedicated to Japan's war dead, stirring a political controversy that has bubbled throughout his four-year term. Yasukuni is controversial because it honors not only civilian victims and regular soldiers from wars dating back to the 19th century, but also more than 1,000 convicted war criminals from World War II, including executed wartime Prime Minister General Hideki Tojo and 13 other class-A war criminals.

Not surprisingly, trips to the shrine by Japanese politicians infuriate countries like China, which was occupied [by Japan] during the war. Mr. Koizumi says his yearly visits are an act of remembrance so as not to repeat the mistakes of war.

While only a radical fringe in Japan still insist that the country's armed forces were wrongly condemned for war atrocities, the debate over Yasukuni highlights one of the noteworthy features of Japan's Shinto religion, which doesn't distinguish between good and evil when it comes to questions of the eternal.

As a pantheist [belief in the ubiquitous presence of divinity] faith, Shinto holds that every object contains a divine spirit, and all aspects of existence have the capacity to be gods. A vast array of shrines dotting the country honor everything from local forests to clocks, snack foods to currency markets.

Because everything is considered divine, those enshrined at Yasukuni are also said to be worthy of religious adulation. "A god doesn't necessarily have to be virtuous," says Yoshinobu Miyake, a Shinto expert at the International Shinto Foundation who also runs a private think tank on religions. The belief that a person's conduct during life is irrelevant to the bestowal of divinity after death has thus been used to explain the enshrinement of war criminals at Yasukuni, he says.

Controversial Political Visits

Former prime ministers Yasuhiro Nakasone in 1985 and Ryutaro Hashimoto in 1996 both caused uproar with their visits to Yasukuni. Koizumi's regular trips drew stern rebukes from both Chinese President Hu Jintao and Premier Wen Jiabao at bilateral summit talks in November [2004], adding tension to a spat over a natural gas field that lies between Japan and China, and the recent incursion of a Chinese nuclear sub into Japanese waters.

Some have suggested that Tokyo could defuse the problem and find a more acceptable way to grieve for

Japanese military officers visit Yasukuni shrine during World War II.

the war dead by "moving" the spirits of the war criminals to an alternate shrine.

But Yasukuni is a religious institution that is independent from the Japanese government. As such, the government has no control over who is enshrined there. Families of Korean and Taiwanese colonial soldiers who fought for Japan during the war have had no success in trying to remove their ancestors from the "Book of Souls" at Yasukuni, which bestows divinity on the war dead. The shrine is notoriously apologetic toward Japan's conduct during the war, saying on its website that the war criminals are martyrs who were "cruelly and unjustly tried . . . by a sham-like tribunal of the Allied forces."

The idea of anyone asking Yasukuni to "move" the spirits also fails to take into account freedom of religion, says Mr. Miyake. "There is no way that public opinion or civic authorities can dictate what an independent religious body should or should not worship— what Yasukuni enshrines is solely the decision of the shrine itself," he says.

Even so, Shinto experts say that such a soul-relocation could be performed. "It would be possible to remove the class-A war criminal from Yasukuni if certain [religious] rituals were undertaken," says Nobutaka Inoue, a professor of Shinto studies at Kokugakuin University. "But the priests at Yasukuni have no such intention."

Others have suggested building a new secular monument to Japan's war dead, but the remaining old soldiers and the families of the deceased are strongly opposed to the idea. "Yasukuni is where all the dead are waiting, no matter what kind of monument they built in another place, the dead wouldn't be there," says Hiromi Kawasaki, who was a mini-sub operator during World War II.

Shinto's Status in Modern Japan Is Uncertain

by Eric Talmadge

In the following article, reporter Eric Talmadge recounts his observations of certain aspects of Shinto belief and practice in contemporary Japan. After talking to a Shinto priest and shrine visitors, he finds that belief in Shinto is declining. Shrines and ceremonies are still important for community activities but even there, and especially among the young, interest is declining. One interviewee goes through the motions of a shrine ritual more out of custom than sincere belief, while many of the visitors to the great shrines at Ise (pronounced "ee-say"), Shinto's most important, are tourists rather than the faithful. It seems that for many Japanese, including priests and members of the emperor's court, Shinto is more an aspect of Japanese history and culture than a religion comparable to Christianity, Islam, or Buddhism.

The steady crowds cross an arched bridge and follow a pebbled path into a forest of towering cypress trees, bowing before a simple gate that stands between them and the holiest place in Japan—the inner sanctuary of the Grand Shrines of Ise.

Though built over a spot believed to pulsate with the

power of the sun goddess, the shrine is weather-beaten and unassuming. It is made entirely of wood, except for a touch of golden gilding on the beams atop its crest. The roof is thatched and covered with patches of moss.

The masses who come to this city on Japan's central coast once would have been called pilgrims. Today, they are mostly just tourists. They offer quick prayers, buy a pocket-size charm or two and head off to their next destination.

Such is the heart of Shinto, Japan's native religion. As old perhaps as Japan itself, Shinto is a rich mixture of folklore, reverence for nature and the Japanese nation itself.

But to say one believes in Shinto has become almost meaningless: The worshipping side of Shinto is relegated to a small cadre of priests and their helpers, most of whom inherited their jobs from ancestors. Most Japanese today "practice" Shinto by making wishes at the local shrine, or enjoying its autumn festivals.

As recently as [World War II], a special brand of state-sanctioned Shinto was the ideological foundation upon which Japan's emperor-worshipping military machine was built. Its treatment of the Japanese people as unique and divine, its emphasis on harmony and its deep-seated fear of impurity continue to be an integral—albeit not always conscious—part of the national psyche.

But stripped of its official status and tarnished by the excesses of militarism, Shinto is struggling to find a place in postwar Japan.

Not Necessarily a Religion

Takashizu Sato comes from a long line of Shinto priests.

"My father, my grandfather, my great-grandfather—

all the way back to feudal times," he said.

Sato went to work for a big company after college. But deciding he needed something more spiritual, he quit, studied for a year, and took up duties at a shrine in the ancient city of Nara. He now works for the Association of Shinto Shrines, to which virtually all Shinto organizations and their 21,000 priests belong.

Like many priests, he hesitates to call Shinto a religion.

"Shinto has no scripture, and no founder," Sato said from the association's Tokyo headquarters. "In that sense, we are very different from the major religions of the world."

But Shinto has no dearth of gods. Its pantheon is poetically said to have 8 million deities, from Amaterasu no Omikami (the sun goddess) to Konohana Sakuya Hime (the goddess of Mount Fuji). That's just a start—all dead ancestors are believed to assume a godlike status.

Along with reverence for the dead and worship of nature, Shinto is built around a complex body of folklore, the most famous of which explains how the Imperial family descended from the sun goddess. Dispelling evil and appeasing the gods are also crucial aspects of Shinto.

Priests don't normally give sermons and congregations don't gather weekly, but Shinto has a strong communal side.

Shrine festivals are big events, and tens of millions of people visit shrines on the first three days of each year. And the country's more than 80,000 shrines—not all have a resident priest—serve as informal neighborhood meeting places, or places for children to play.

"It's difficult to pin down, but there is something about Shinto that is very fundamental to the Japanese mentality," Sato said.

Even so, the ties between Shinto—the faith—and the average people are weakening.

The tightknit communities that once kept shrines alive are unraveling, many young people at festivals are more interested in fun than religion, and the small Shinto altars once common in homes are disappearing.

"We still look Japanese, but inside we are forgetting what that means," Sato said. "It's our responsibility to try to revive what makes us Japanese."

Emperor Denies Being a God

After World War II, the late Emperor Showa changed the state's role in Shinto when—at the behest of Allied Occupation forces—he publicly renounced the idea that he was a living god. A new Constitution was enacted that ensured freedom of religion and the separation of church and state.

These days, Shinto pamphlets intended for foreign audiences stress the faith's respect for the environment—yet Shinto's basic tenets still haven't changed much.

The personal priests of today's Emperor Akihito still observe Shinto rituals at three shrines behind the Imperial Palace, and not far away lies the site of a vociferous dispute over Shinto's place in Japanese culture, Yasukuni Shrine.

Synonymous with nationalism, Yasukuni was built in the late 1800s as a monument to Japan's military might and a memorial to its fallen soldiers. Howls of outrage from across Asia and several constitutional challenges to official patronage have not stopped political leaders from regularly bowing before its altar.

One who objects to the official visits is Tadashi Mizoguchi, whose brother is one of the 2.5 million dead soldiers enshrined at Yasukuni.

"We both fought in World War II," Mizoguchi said. "Through the grace of God, I was spared. But he was killed in Taiwan."

Mizoguchi converted to Christianity and began to question the wartime beliefs that justified his battlefield actions. Today, he bristles at the idea that all Japanese, by birth, belong to Shinto, and he wants his brother removed from the Yasukuni pantheon.

"How can they make him a god? There is only one God," Mizoguchi said. "They are using him—even in death."

Lip Service for Good Luck

Still, Shinto plays a role in Japanese life. Akie Ishiguro and her husband, Takashi, toss a few coins into a collection box, ring a big bronze bell and bow their heads in prayer.

With their first baby due, they've come to a popular haven for pregnant women, Tokyo's Suitengu Shrine, which legend says can promise an easy birth to a woman given a piece of the cloth hanging from the shrine's bell.

Akie Ishiguro said she and her husband "really don't believe" in any of that.

"It's just something that we Japanese people do," she said. "It's kind of an event, a tradition."

"And you never know," she said. "If there's something that I can do to help ensure that my baby will be born healthy, it's worth a try."

Glossary

Amaterasu: Shinto sun goddess.

aramitama: The harsh, violent aspect of each Shinto *kami.*

bodhisattva: A "little Buddha," or enlightened soul, who chooses to remain among humans to help them achieve enlightenment. Many bodhisattvas are also considered Shinto deities.

Buddhism: A major religion in Japan and around the world based on the belief that one needs to follow the dharma, or proper path, to achieve enlightenment, or freedom from the sufferings of the world.

Confucianism: A school of thought imported to Japan from China. It emphasizes social harmony, an earthly hierarchy recognized through rituals, and filial piety.

Daikokuten: The *kami* of wealth and prosperity.

Engishiki: The first published book of Shinto rites, from the tenth century.

gohei: Strips of paper that symbolize the presence of *kami* at shrines or during rituals.

guji: A shrine's chief priest.

Hachiman: A Shinto rice deity of war and battle.

harae: Shinto purification rituals.

Inari: A popular Shinto deity often associated with the fox.

Ise: Shinto's main shrine. The sun goddess Amaterasu is worshipped in its inner shrine while the outer shrine is devoted to the harvest deity Toyouke.

Izanagi: "He who invites," the male creator of Japan and father of the first deities.

Izanami: "She who invites," the female creator of Japan and mother of the first deities.

Izumo: The name for an area and clan important in early Japan. The Izumo shrine is second only in importance to Ise in historical Shinto.

Jimmu Tenno: The legendary first emperor of Japan and founder of the still-existing imperial line in approximately 660 B.C.

jinja: A Shinto shrine.

kami: Shinto gods or spirits.

kamidama: A household altar.

kamikaze: A divine wind.

kannushi: A shinto priest.

Kojiki: The earliest written Japanese chronicle, dating to 712.

Kokka Shinto: The state-directed Shinto of the imperialist era, 1868–1945.

matsuri: A festival.

Meiji Restoration: The installation of the Meiji emporer in 1868 by political reformers seeking to modernize Japan. The term is sometimes used to encompass the period lasting until 1945, even though the Meiji emporer was succeeded in 1912 by the Taisho emporer, who was in turn succeeded in 1926 by the Showa emporer.

miko: A female shrine attendant.

mikoshi: A portable Shinto shrine used in religious parades.

misogi: Purification by water.

myojin: A Buddhist term for Shinto *kami*.

nigimatama: The kind, benevolent aspect of each Shinto *kami.*

Nihongi: Also known as *Nihon shoki;* the second-oldest written chronicle of Japan.

norito: Shinto prayers or liturgies.

sakaki: A tree whose branches are commonly used in Shinto rites.

shinbutsu shugo: The interaction of Shinto and Buddhism.

shinkoku: "Divine country"; the idea that the Japanese nation is protected by the Shinto *kami.*

Susano: Shinto storm god.

tama: The vital force of Shinto *kami.*

Taoism (sometimes spelled Daoism): A Chinese religion imported to Japan. It focuses on spiritual harmony with nature and the universe.

torii: The gateway to a shrine, signifying the border between the sacred and the earthly.

Toyouke: A Shinto goddess of the harvest and other natural bounties.

Tsukiyomi: Shinto moon god.

ujigami: A guardian family deity.

wa: Benign harmony.

waka: A thirty-one-syllable Japanese poem also known as *tanka.*

Yamato: Japan's ruling clan during the Nara period (710–794).

Yomi: The Shinto land of the dead.

Chronology

B.C.
660–585
The reign of Jimmu Tenno, legendary first emperor of Japan.

250
The beginning of the Yayoi period of Japanese history (250 B.C.–A.D. 250), when people created the concept of the *kami* to explain the divine force that animates life and nature.

97
According to the chronicle *Nihongi*, the emperor Sujin established the difference between heavenly and earthly *kami*. Legends also proclaim that the Ise shrine was established.

A.D.
100–250
The earliest forms of Shinto emerge under Yamato clan leaders.

400–600
Chinese influences arrive in Japan, often via Korean intermediaries. These include Chinese writing and the religions of Confucianism, Taoism, and Buddhism.

580
According to the *Nihongi*, the emperor Yomei professes both Shinto and Buddhism.

672

Emperor Temmu begins the custom of rebuilding the Ise shrine every twenty years.

710–794

The Nara period of Japanese history, characterized by the first written records, the continued dominance of the Yamato clan, and the integration of Shintoism and Buddhism. Leaders devise the word *Shinto* (from the Chinese *shen-dao*, or "way of the gods"), to differentiate Shinto from Buddhism.

712

Japan's earliest written chronicle, the *Kojiki*, is completed.

720

The *Nihongi*, also known as *Nihon shoki*, is completed.

794

The beginning of the Heian period of Japanese history (794–1185). Leaders transfer the nation's capital to Kyoto to avoid Buddhist- or Chinese-influenced political meddlers.

927

The *Engishiki*, a collection of liturgies and prayers, is completed.

1185

The beginning of the Kamakura period (1185–1333) of Japanese history, so named because Kamakura is the city to which Japan's new rulers, the Minamoto clan, move the nation's capital. It is the first of several eras in which Japan is dominated politically by shoguns rather than emperors. The word *shogun* might be translated as "emperor's military adviser." The first shogun, Minamoto Yoritomo, takes the title in 1192. The emperor's court, meanwhile, remains in Kyoto. The emperor Antoku dies at sea, losing the imperial sword.

It soon becomes customary to associate the imperial line with three objects: a sword, a jewel, and a mirror. All are invested with Shinto significance.

1222–1282
The life of the Buddhist reformer Nichiren. His work reinvigorates Shinto as well.

1274
Kublai Khan and the Mongols attempt their first invasion of Japan.

1281
The second attempted Mongol invasion. As with the first, this invasion is turned back by storms which are denoted kamikaze, or "divine winds."

1336
The beginning of the Ashikaga period of Japanese history (1336–1573), named for the new dominant clan. It is also known as the Muromachi period since the shogunal family resides in a district of Kyoto known as Muromachi.

1462
The state, due to severe financial problems, abandons its economic support of the main Shinto shrines, a custom that had dated back to the Heian era.

1467
The beginning of the so-called "century of the country at war," when Japan was in constant conflict among dominant clans, bands of samurai warriors, and militant Buddhist monks.

1549
Missionary Francis Xavier introduces Roman Catholic Christianity to Japan.

1576–1598
Japan is reunited and made mostly peaceful under the warlords Oda Nobunaga (1534–1582) and Toyotomi Hideyoshi (1536–1598).

1600–1868
The period of the Tokugawa shogunate. It begins when Tokugawa Ieyasu inherits the role of warlord from Toyotomi and is designated shogun.

1639
European merchant and missionary activity is banned completely by Tokugawa authorities. They allow only two Dutch ships per year to dock at Nagasaki. All Japanese Christians, meanwhile, are forced to recant.

1776–1843
The life of Hirata Atsutane, the leading figure in the Shinto restoration movement of the early 1800s.

1853
American navy commodore Matthew Perry arrives in Japan with demands for trading and other privileges. Tokugawa leaders have no choice but to submit.

1867
The last Tokugawa shogun, Yoshinobu, abdicates in favor of a group of young samurai who advocate Japan's modernization. The reformers install Mutsuhito as the new emperor, beginning the Meiji period of Japanese history (1868–1912).

1868
Japan's reformers restore Shinto as the guiding religion of the Japanese state. In March they officially separate Shinto from Buddhism.

1869

The new government creates several state offices for Shinto, including one for propaganda asserting the centrality of Shinto to the nation.

1871

Shinto shrines are declared national institutions. Many Shinto priests receive paychecks as civil servants.

1889

The new Japanese constitution recognizes Shinto, Buddhism, and Confucianism as official, but separate, religions.

1900

The Bureau of Shinto Affairs is established by the Japanese government to further entrench Shinto as the "national way."

1912

The death of the Meiji emperor. He is replaced by Yoshihito, the Taisho emperor.

1921

The Meiji shrine in Tokyo is completed to honor the deified Meiji emperor.

1926

At the death of the Taisho emperor, Showa emperor Hirohito accedes to the throne.

1931

Japan invades Manchuria, north of China, and after victory sets up Manchukuo, a puppet state.

1937

Japan invades China, beginning World War II in Asia.

1940

Japan celebrates the twenty-six-hundredth anniversary of the accession of the first emperor, Jimmu Tenno. It is an occasion for Shinto-based nationalism.

1941

On December 7 Japanese warplanes conduct a surprise attack on the American naval base at Pearl Harbor, Hawaii, bringing the United States into World War II.

1945

August. Japan loses World War II. Hirohito announces the surrender over the radio on August 15. U.S. Army general Douglas MacArthur is installed as the supreme commander of Allied forces in occupied Japan.
December. American occupation authorities issue the Shinto Directive, dismantling state Shinto.

1946

Hirohito publicly announces that neither he nor any other Japanese emperor is divine.

1952

The American occupation ends.

1985

The first Shinto shrine built outside Japan since 1945 appears in Stockton, California. During the Meiji era, shrines were built by Japanese immigrants in both Hawaii and Brazil.

1989

Hirohito, the Showa emperor, dies. He is replaced by Akihito, the Heisei emperor and current holder of the sacred mirror, sword, and jewel.

1993

The most recent rebuilding of the Ise shrine, the sixty-sixth.

1996

The two-thousandth anniversary of the Ise shrine is celebrated.

1998

The first online Shinto shrine, Sakura Jinja, is established.

For Further Research

Books

Michael Ashkenazi, *Matsuri: Festivals of a Japanese Town.* Honolulu: University of Hawaii Press, 1993.

W.G. Aston, trans., *Nihongi: Chronicles of Japan from the Earliest Times.* London: George Allen & Unwin Ltd., 1896.

Robert N. Bellah, *Tokugawa Religion: The Cultural Roots of Modern Japan.* New York: Free Press, 1957.

Felicia Grisset Bock, trans., *Engi-Shiki: Procedures of the Engi Era.* Books 6–10. Tokyo: Sophia University, 1972.

John Breen and Mark Teeuwen, eds., *Shinto in History: Ways of the Kami.* Honolulu: University of Hawaii Press, 2000.

Jan van Bremen and D.P. Martinez, eds., *Ceremony and Ritual in Japan: Religious Practices in an Industrialized Society.* London: Routledge, 1995.

William K. Bunce, *Religions in Japan: Buddhism, Shinto, Christianity.* Rutland, VT: Charles E. Tuttle, 1955.

W. Davis, *Japanese Religion and Society: Paradigms of Structural Change.* Albany: State University of New York Press, 1992.

H. Byron Earhart, *Japanese Religion: Unity and Diversity.* 3rd ed. Belmont, CA: Wadsworth, 1982.

George Elison and Bardwell L. Smith, eds., *Warlords, Artists, and Commoners: Japan in the Sixteenth Century.* Honolulu: University of Hawaii Press, 1981.

Louis Frederic, *Daily Life in Japan at the Time of the Samurai,*

1185–1603. Trans. Eileen M. Lowe. London: George Allen & Unwin Ltd., 1972.

Helen Hardacre, *Shinto and the State, 1868–1988*. Princeton, NJ: Princeton University Press, 1989.

William Horsley and Roger Buckley, *Nippon, New Superpower: Japan Since 1945*. London: BBC Books, 1990.

Engelbert Kaempfer, *Kaempfer's Japan: Tokugawa Culture Observed*. Ed. and trans. Beatrice M. Bodart-Bailey. Honolulu: University of Hawaii Press, 1999.

Tadaaki Kurozomi and Isshi Kohmoto, *The Living Way: Stories of Kurozomi Munetada, a Shinto Founder*. Trans. Sumio Kamiya. Ed. Willis Stoesz. Walnut Creek, CA: Altamira, 1999.

C. Scott Littleton, *Shinto*. Oxford, UK: Oxford University Press, 2002.

Peter Martin, *The Chrysanthemum Throne: A History of the Emperors of Japan*. Honolulu: University of Hawaii Press, 1997.

Anesaki Masaharu, *Japanese Mythology*. New York: Cooper Square, 1964.

John K. Nelson, *Enduring Identities: The Guise of Shinto in Contemporary Japan*. Honolulu: University of Hawaii Press, 2000.

———, *A Year in the Life of a Shinto Shrine*. Seattle: University of Washington Press, 1996.

Stuart D.B. Picken, *Historical Dictionary of Shinto*. Lanham, MD: Scarecrow, 2002.

Juliet Piggott, *Japanese Mythology*. London: Hamlyn, 1969.

Ian Reader, *Religion in Contemporary Japan*. Honolulu: University of Hawaii Press, 1991.

Edwin O. Reischauer, *Japan: The Story of a Nation*. 3rd ed. New York: Alfred A. Knopf, 1981.

Conrad Schirokauer, *A Brief History of Chinese and Japanese Civilizations.* San Diego, CA: Harcourt Brace Jovanovich, 1989.

Murakami Shigeyoshi, *Japanese Religion in the Modern Century.* Tokyo: University of Tokyo Press, 1980.

Karen A. Smyers, *The Fox and the Jewel: Shared and Private Meanings in Contemporary Japanese Inari Worship.* Honolulu: University of Hawaii Press, 1999.

Muraoka Tsunetsugu, *Studies in Shinto Thought.* Trans. Delmer M. Brown and James T. Araki. Westport, CT: Greenwood, 1964.

Stephen Turnbull, *Samurai Warriors.* London: Blandford, 1987.

Michiko Yusa, *Japanese Religious Traditions.* Upper Saddle River, NJ: Prentice Hall, 2002.

Periodicals

H. Anderson, "Japan's Sacred Rice God," *Newsweek*, October 17, 1988.

James W. Boyd and Ray G. Williams, "Japanese Shinto: An Interpretation of a Priestly Perspective," *Philosophy East and West*, January 2005.

Christian Century, "Dispute over Shintoism," December 11, 1991.

Florian Coulmas, "Eternal Change at the Grand Shrine of Ise," *Japan Quarterly*, January–March 1994.

Howard W. French, "Japan Has Little Time for its Old-Time Religion," *New York Times*, September 13, 2001.

R. Schlender and Takeshi Yuzawa, "What Rice Means to the Japanese," *Fortune*, November 1, 1993.

Stephanie Strom, "Japan's Premier Visits War Shrine, Pleasing Few," *New York Times*, August 14, 2001.

Web Sites

Cyber Shrine, www.kiku.com/electric_samurai/cyber_shrine. Links to photos of many of Japan's major shrines.

Hawaii Korahiru Jinshu, www.e-shrine.org. The Web site of a Shinto shrine in Hawaii. Provides many links to other Shinto resources.

Japan Guide, www.japan-guide.com. General informational site on Japan with a large section on Shinto. Provides information on shrines, daily life, and the arts. Many photos.

ReligiousTolerance.Org, www.religioustolerance.org/shinto.htm. General description of Shinto history and practice organized in outline form.

Shinto Online Network Association, www.jinja.org.jp. Provides basic definitions, a historical overview, descriptions of Shinto sects, and photos.

Index